PRACTICAL ART ANATOMY

PRACTICAL
ART ANATOMY

BY

E. G. LUTZ
AUTHOR OF "PRACTICAL DRAWING," ETC.

WITH ILLUSTRATIONS BY THE AUTHOR

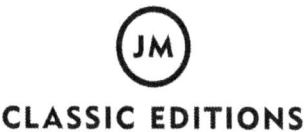

CLASSIC EDITIONS

This edition digitally re-mastered and
published by JM Classic Editions © 2007
Original text © E G Lutz 1918

ISBN 978-1-905217-85-4

CONTENTS

PART ONE

THE FRAMEWORK OF THE BODY

CHAPTER I. THE SKELETON

CHAPTER II. THE AXIAL SKELETON

CHAPTER III. THE CRANIAL SKELETON
(CONTINUING THE AXIAL SKELETON)

CHAPTER IV. THE SKELETON OF THE UPPER LIMB

CHAPTER V. THE SKELETON OF THE LOWER LIMB

PART TWO

THE GENERAL FORM OF THE BODY

CHAPTER VI. THE MUSCULAR SYSTEM

CHAPTER VII. THE MUSCLES OF THE TRUNK

CHAPTER VIII. THE MUSCLES OF THE HEAD AND THE NECK

CHAPTER IX. THE MUSCLES OF THE UPPER LIMB

CHAPTER X. THE MUSCLES OF THE LOWER LIMB

PART ONE

THE FRAMEWORK OF THE BODY

I

THE SKELETON

THE SKELETON IN GENERAL—THE FOUR KINDS OF BONES

THE skeleton is that part of the physical organism that gives fixedness and stability in repose and constitutes in activity the hard portions of the apparatus of movement and locomotion. Or putting it concisely: the skeleton is the framework of the body.

This framework, however, besides sustaining the figure when it is in repose, and becoming a piece of mechanism during movement, also protects and furnishes areas of support for soft tissues and delicate organs of the body. The bony cage of the chest and the pelvic basin, for instance, contain and shield organs of the trunk.

Again, it is to the bones that the larger muscles, the active elements of power that move this mechanism, find their points of attachment.

Anatomists have grouped the different kinds of bones of the human skeleton into four classes: flat, long, short, and irregular. The bones forming the pelvic basin are flat bones. The shoulder-blade and breast-bone are likewise placed under this grouping. The cranium, so often referred to by scientific writers as the brain-box, is formed, in the main, from a

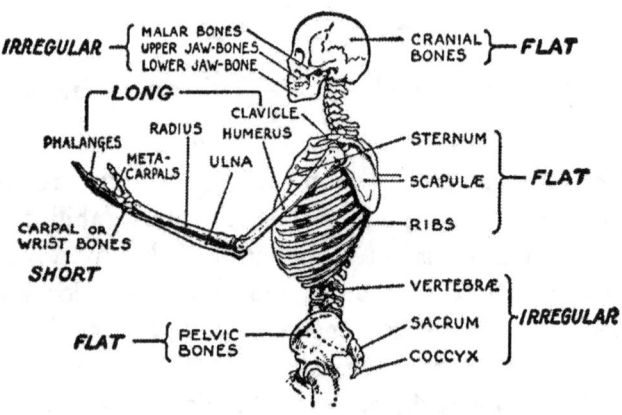

DIAGRAM TO ILLUSTRATE THE FOUR CLASSES OF BONES.

number of flat bones. The names and the positions of the principal ones will be noted farther on when the skeleton of the head is taken up.

Long bones, a very important class, make up the structural support of the limbs. Of this kind, there are found in the upper arm, the humerus; and in the forearm, the radius and the ulna. The skeletal part of the first section of the lower limb, the thigh, like the first section of the arm, contains but one bone, the femur. In the second section again, the leg, there are two long bones, the tibia and the fibula. The bones of the palm, or body of the hand, those of the digits; the principal segments forming the bony arch of the foot, and the bones of the toes, come under the designation of long bones. The collar-bone is a long bone, too.

The short bones are exemplified by the skeletal segments of the wrist and ankle. The knee-pan, or patella, which functionally is looked upon as a sesamoid, or pulley-bone, is considered as a short bone.

Of the irregular bones, the fourth class, the most significant are the serial divisions of the back-bone. They are the vertebræ. The two lowermost portions of the back-bone, the sacrum and the coccyx, are also irregular bones. Nearly all the facial bones and some of the basilar cranial bony pieces are placed with the irregular bones.

THE ARTICULATIONS: IMMOVABLE AND MOVABLE —MIXED ARTICULATIONS

The combining of the various bones to complete the entire skeleton is effected by joints, or articulations. As a general classification, the articulations are designated as either movable or immovable. In the head where the edges of the bones are closely united by dovetail fittings, the articulations are of the immovable kind. The irregular, zigzagging fis-

sures to be seen on a skull are typical examples of
immovable joints.   They are called sutures.

In certain other joinings of bones, as that of the
union, in the front, of the two pelvic bones, and in

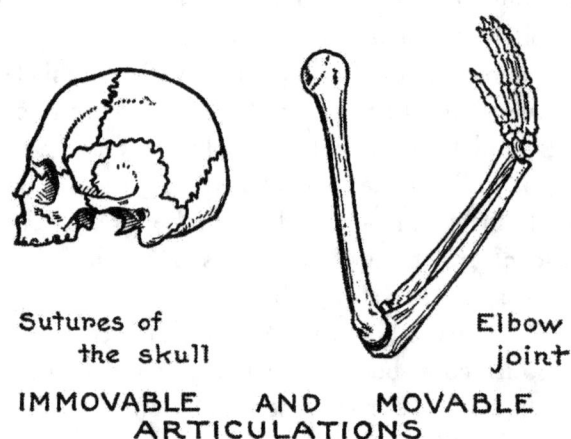

Sutures of
the skull

Elbow
joint

IMMOVABLE   AND   MOVABLE
ARTICULATIONS

the series of vertebræ in the back-bone, there is an
indeterminate amount of movement.   These joints
are regarded as mixed articulations as they have
but limited mobility.

But of significance to the artist, as a matter of
practical knowledge, is that form of articulation
known as the perfect, or movable, joint.   This type
is exemplified in the linking of the extremities to the
trunk and in the joining of their separate sections.

The several kinds of movable articulations are named according to their resemblance, in form and function, to certain mechanistic structures and movements.

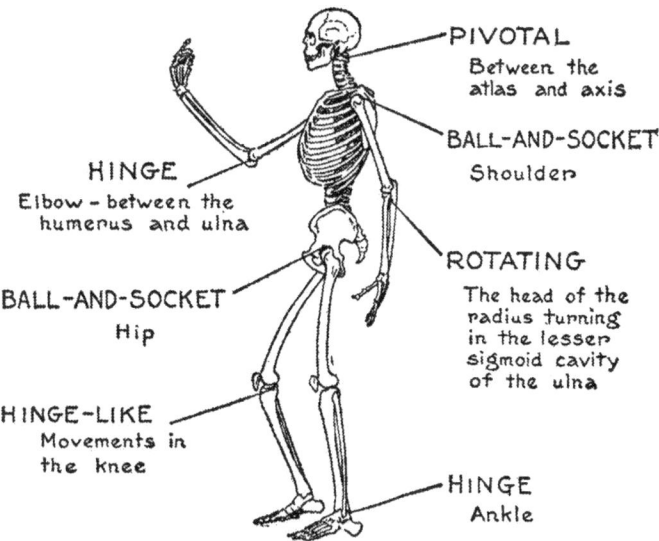

PIVOTAL
Between the atlas and axis

BALL-AND-SOCKET
Shoulder

HINGE
Elbow - between the humerus and ulna

ROTATING
The head of the radius turning in the lesser sigmoid cavity of the ulna

BALL-AND-SOCKET
Hip

HINGE-LIKE
Movements in the knee

HINGE
Ankle

ARTICULATIONS OF THE SKELETON ILLUSTRATING VARIOUS KINDS OF MECHANICAL JOINTS AND MOVEMENTS.

Of the different kinds, the first in interest is the ball-and-socket joint. There are two good examples of this type of joint in the human framework: in the shoulder and in the hip. The hip-joint is, perhaps, the most machine-like contrivance in the whole skeleton. The joint cavity of the hip-bone is deep and cup-like, and it receives with almost perfect adjustment the spherical head of the thigh-bone.

In the shoulder, considered as a mere mechanism, the parts do not approach so closely to the ball-and-socket idea. The head of the upper-arm bone is approximately globular, but the socket on the blade-bone is shallow. When the shoulder-joint, though, is completed with its enclosing fibrous capsule and ligaments, it forms in function a good example of this ball-and-socket type.

The articulation at the elbow is a hinge-joint. The movement, too, is distinctly hinge-like; that is, the play of movement is in one plane only, forward and backward. Although as a matter of construction, the bones in the knee and the ankle are not arranged as in a hinge, the articulations are known as hinge-joints, as the parts concerned move mainly in one plane—forward and backward.

In the forearm, the fashion in which the wheel-like head of the radius turns in a depression on its neighboring bone, the ulna, is also of a pivotal nature. This joint may also be described as a rotating one, as it causes, when functioning, a rotatory movement to the radius.

An interesting articulation is the pivoting one of the first and second vertebræ. Here the first vertebra, the atlas (the globular skull rests on it) has a notch which fits around a tooth-like projection of the second vertebra. This second vertebra is the axis, and it is around its bony tooth, or pivot, that most of the turning of the head from side to side takes place.

The peculiarity of the adjustment of two bones

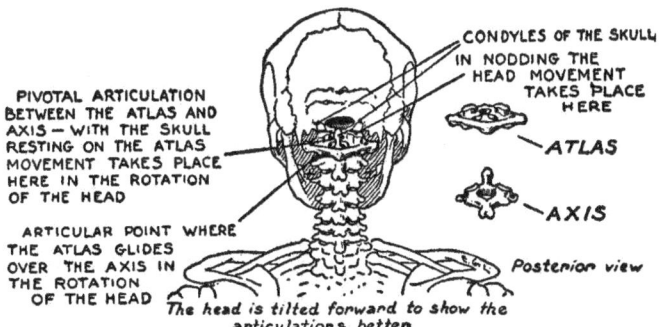

PIVOTAL ARTICULATION BETWEEN THE ATLAS AND AXIS — WITH THE SKULL RESTING ON THE ATLAS MOVEMENT TAKES PLACE HERE IN THE ROTATION OF THE HEAD

ARTICULAR POINT WHERE THE ATLAS GLIDES OVER THE AXIS IN THE ROTATION OF THE HEAD

CONDYLES OF THE SKULL IN NODDING THE HEAD MOVEMENT TAKES PLACE HERE

ATLAS

AXIS

Posterior view

The head is tilted forward to show the articulations better

DIAGRAM TO SHOW HOW THE HEAD MOVES ON TOP OF THE SPINAL COLUMN.

taking part in a movable joint is, in general, that one bone has a convex surface fitting into a concave one of the other. In some cases the convexity is but slight, and the corresponding depression very shallow, as in the different wrist and some of the ankle bones. In such articulations, the direction of the movement may be hinge-like, or even rotatory, but the joints are generally spoken of as gliding ones.

The Ligaments

The articulated bones of the skeleton are held together at their points of contact by ligamentous cords or bands. In most cases the important ligaments pass from bone to bone, laterally to the joint, so as not to interfere with the play of activity intended for that particular place. Certain ligaments, too, besides holding the articular surfaces at their proper relationship, act as check ligaments to keep the range of movement from going too far, or in the wrong direction. Some articulations, especially those that are put frequently into action, are further strengthened by additional parts called capsular ligaments or joint capsules. One such is a sort of bag completely surrounding the joint. They are well exemplified in the joints of the shoulder and hip.

It is to be kept in mind that the whole assemblage of bones with their articulations, ligaments, and certain cartilaginous portions complete, from an artist's point of view, the framework of the body. To him it is the apparatus of movement, the structure that gives the fundamentals of equilibrium in a pose, and the frame on which the soft form-filling parts are laid.

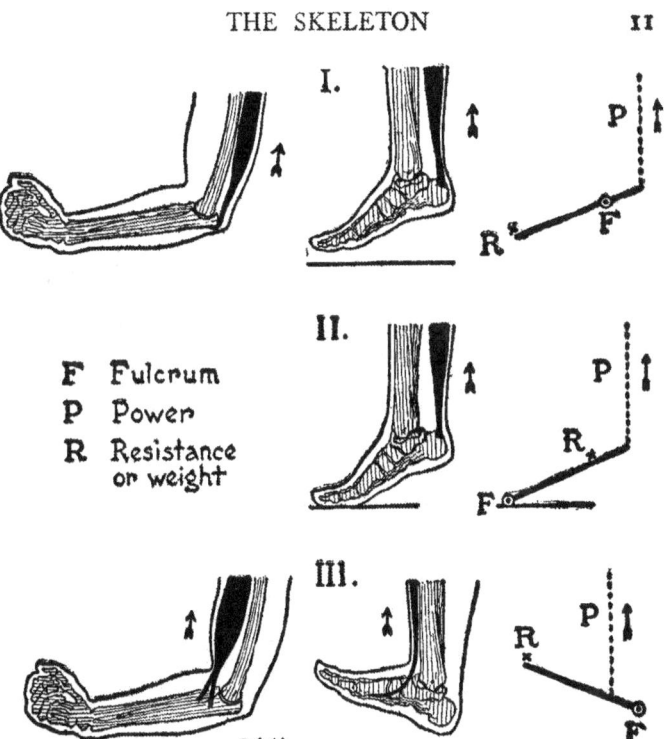

I.

II.

F Fulcrum
P Power
R Resistance
  or weight

III.

EXAMPLES IN THE HUMAN STRUCTURE OF THE THREE ORDERS
OF LEVERS.

THE BONY LEVERS

We apprehend by a general glance at the skeleton that many of the bones in their arrangements take the form of levers. Particularly is this in evidence in the long bones concerned in locomotion, or motion involving great activity, or the doing of definite or practical things. All three classes of levers are exhibited in the human osseous structure.

The first class of levers, where the fulcrum is placed between the weight and the power, is instanced in the arm when the muscle on the back of the upper arm pulls on the projection of the forearm bone at the back of the elbow to straighten out the limb. And again in the leg when the calf muscles pull the heel-bone to move the foot.

In the second class of levers, the resistance, or weight, is found between the power and the fulcrum. When we stand on our toes the disposition of the skeletal parts of the foot and leg takes the form of this type of lever. The weight of our body —the resistance—bearing down at the ankle-joint, comes between the fulcrum—the ground where the toes touch—and the power—the contracting calf muscles.

In the third class of levers the power is applied between the fulcrum and the resistance. This type is illustrated in bending the elbow. The elbow joint is the fulcrum, the hand the weight, and the biceps muscle pulling on the forearm bone is the power. Again when the foot is lifted free from the ground and then flexed we have another example of the third class of levers. In this case the muscles of the front of the leg—the power—exert their force on the skeleton of the foot immediately in front of the ankle-joint—the fulcrum. The tip of the toes represents the resistance.

THE HELPFULNESS IN DRAWING OF AN UNDERSTANDING OF THE SKELETON

Before we go on with the study of the separate segments composing the bony framework, it will be well to set forth some of the reasons for giving our attention, as artists, to such study.

Thus, when ascertaining the general proportions of the figure, only the bones with their hard subcutaneous surfaces furnish any sort of reliable, fixed points for measurements. And the bones, too, give the best suggestions where to mark construction lines in the preliminary sketching when establishing the pose, or for work depicting action. For character drawing and portraiture, the skeletal indications of the head that show outwardly are important matters to study and seriously to consider, so as to interpret intelligently the particular visage to be portrayed. It would help, again, in drawing the trunk, to have a good understanding of the construction of the bony thorax and the shape of the pelvis, as they can be considered as fixed and rigid formations. They take a great part in determining the outer form as it presents itself to the eye.

Then there are throughout the figure important

landmarks where parts of the bones become sub-cutaneous, that is, they have these parts close under the skin, and so directly influence the form. The subcutaneous surface of the tibia, or shin-bone, is a good example of such a bony landmark.

Another point, to mention it again, is that it is to the bones, in nearly all cases, that muscles find their points of attachment. So it is obviously clear, then, that some knowledge of the bones is necessary as a fundamental in the study of the muscular system.

The Order of Our Study of the Skeleton

It remains now to refer to the order in which we will study the osseous structure of the body.

First we begin with what the anatomists describe as the axial skeleton, the primary element of which is the spine, or back-bone. After we have given our attention to this part we will continue with the bones of its cojoined parts, the thorax and the pelvis. The consideration of the bones of the cranium and face, also forming parts of the axial skeleton, completes our study of this, the primary division of the osseous framework.

Next in order are the bones of the limbs, or the appendicular portions of the skeleton. Naturally we begin with the upper, and then go on with the lower limb. The attention should be directed to the homology, or relative sameness, of the structural plan in which the respective segments of the two limbs are arranged.

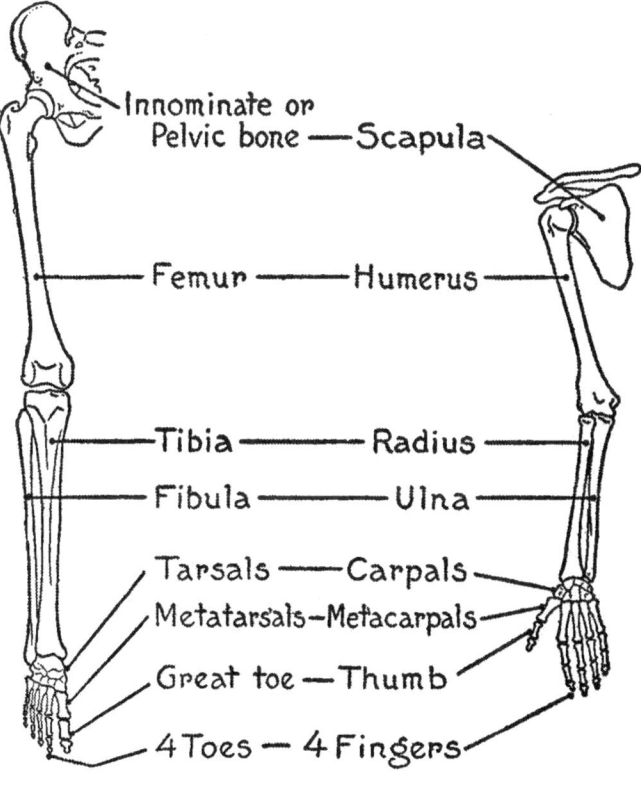

Innominate or
Pelvic bone —— Scapula
Femur —— Humerus
Tibia —— Radius
Fibula —— Ulna
Tarsals —— Carpals
Metatarsals — Metacarpals
Great toe — Thumb
4 Toes — 4 Fingers

SIMILARITY OF THE STRUCTURAL PLAN IN THE TWO LIMBS.

II

THE AXIAL SKELETON

THE SPINAL COLUMN—ITS BONY SEGMENTS OR VERTEBRÆ

THE spinal column, the middle division of the axial skeleton, is a flexible strong stem to which the other osseous parts of the body are attached. It is the bony chain, it may be said, that links the rest of the frame together. In drawing from life, a line to represent it may not always be the first thing to mark on the paper, but the direction of its curve is, at least, the first thing to take note of and reflect upon. The trend of its curve influences the movement, action, or pose of the entire figure.

Besides the term already used, this part of the bony structure is called the vertebral column, the spine, or simply the back-bone.

The spinal column is composed of a number of connected segments forming a more or less easily bent stem. Each separate segment of the series is called a vertebra. An opening in each vertebra, the spinal foramen, forms with the corresponding foramina of the other vertebræ, a long canal through

which the spinal cord passes. With the exception
of the atlas, each of the vertebræ has a thick part
called the body, back of which is a ring, or arch,
that forms the opening spoken of immediately

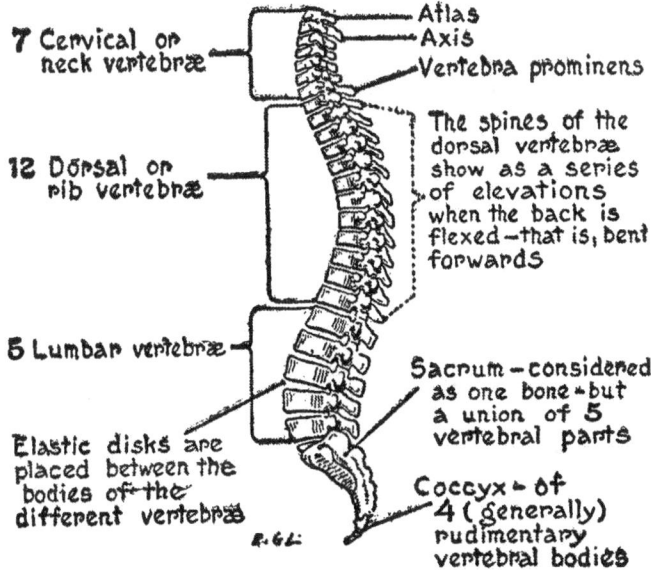

7 Cervical or
neck vertebræ

Atlas
Axis
Vertebra prominens

The spines of the
dorsal vertebræ
show as a series
of elevations
when the back is
flexed—that is, bent
forwards

12 Dorsal or
rib vertebræ

5 Lumbar vertebræ

Sacrum—considered
as one bone—but
a union of 5
vertebral parts

Elastic disks are
placed between the
bodies of the
different vertebræ

Coccyx—of
4 (generally)
rudimentary
vertebral bodies

R. G. L.

THE SPINAL COLUMN AND ITS DIVISIONS.

above. From the body of a vertebra and its arch
there are several processes, or projections of bone.
The lateral ones are the transverse processes, while
the single one, placed posteriorly and pointing backward, and in most of them downward, is a spinous
process. These spinous processes, or neural spines,

are of especial significance. They show in the certain parts of the length of the spinal column as a series of knobs when the back is bent.

It would be well at this point to take note of

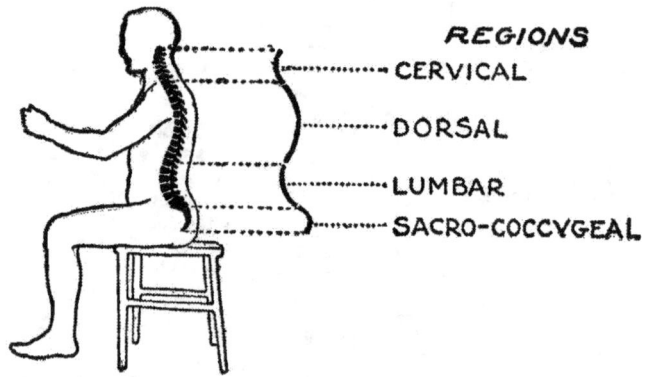

REGIONS

CERVICAL

DORSAL

LUMBAR

SACRO-COCCYGEAL

THE SUCCESSION OF CONTRASTING CURVES IN THE SPINAL COLUMN.

the meaning of the word "process" as it is used in the study of the skeleton. The term designates an outgrowth, jutting out very conspicuously, from the general body of a bone.

The Three Kinds of Vertebræ

In man the number of vertebræ composing the back-bone is twenty-four. Below the lowest of these there are two bony portions formed of modified or rudimentary vertebræ. The first portion is the sacrum, an immovable union of five vertebral parts, the other is the coccyx of four (usually) rudimen-

tary vertebræ.   Anatomists include the sacrum and
the coccyx as forming part of the back-bone; if
counted in, the five sacral and four coccygeal seg-

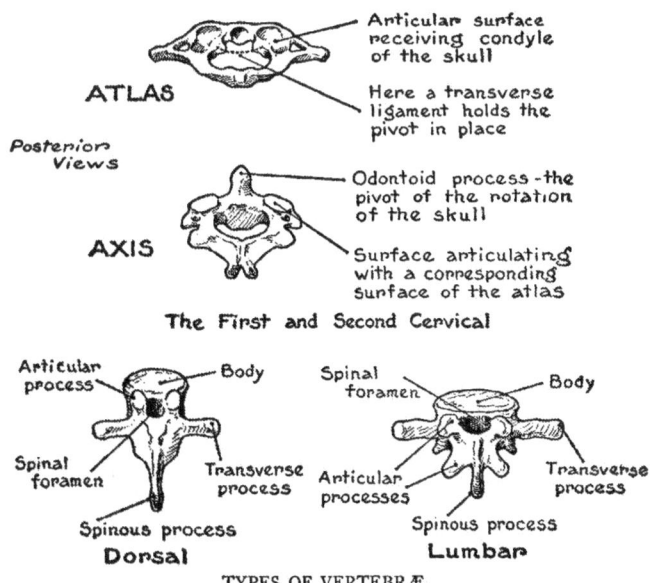

ATLAS

Articular surface
receiving condyle
of the skull

Here a transverse
ligament holds the
pivot in place

Posterior
Views

AXIS

Odontoid process - the
pivot of the rotation
of the skull

Surface articulating
with a corresponding
surface of the atlas

The First and Second Cervical

Articular
process

Body

Spinal
foramen

Transverse
process

Spinous process
Dorsal

Spinal
foramen

Body

Anticular
processes

Transverse
process

Spinous process
Lumbar

TYPES OF VERTEBRÆ.

ments would make the number of the vertebral
parts constituting the whole column as thirty-three.
   But it is enough for the artist to regard as the
spinal column proper only that section comprising
the twenty-four movable vertebræ.   It may be
noted here that very few back-bone animals have
fewer vertebral parts than man, and that they

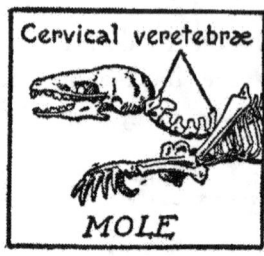

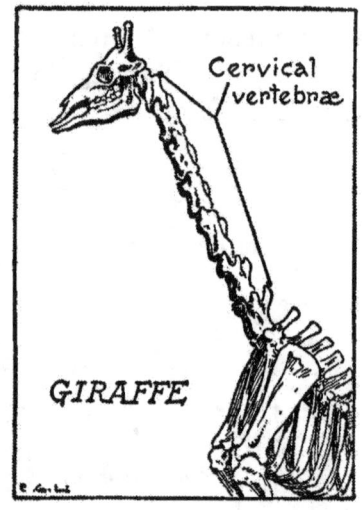

In all the mammalian animals, with but a few exceptions, the number of cervical vertebræ is constant: namely, seven.

usually have many more. In fishes and reptiles several hundred, for instance.

Of the twenty-four human vertebræ there are seven cervical, or those of the neck; twelve dorsal, or thoracic, and five lumbar.

The first series, the cervical, bring to the attention a very curious detail of natural science. It is this: In all mammalian animals, with but a few exceptions, the neck vertebræ number seven. In the long neck of the giraffe, for instance, there are but seven vertebræ, and in animals that appear to have no neck at all there are likewise seven. The exceptions occur in one of the species of manatees, or seacows, and certain species of sloths.

The first cervical vertebra, the atlas, and the second, the axis, on which the atlas turns, have already been referred to in the preceding chapter. Their articular arrangement with the corresponding bearing parts of the skull and the completion of ligamentous parts form the mechanism by which the head moves up and down, and turns from side to side. The "yes" and "no" movements, it might be said.

The last, or seventh, cervical vertebra is called the vertebra prominens, because it forms a conspicuous elevation at the back of the neck where a man's collar-stud sometimes rubs against the skin.

The next group of spinal segments, the middle division, is that of the twelve dorsal vertebræ. To them are joined the twelve pairs of ribs. For this reason they are also called the rib vertebræ.

The third group is that of the five lumbar vertebræ, or those of the loins. They are the largest of the vertebral segments.

The vertebræ of the dorsal region have the longest spinous processes, and they are longest, too, as a rule, in animals. The immense hump of the American bison, or buffalo, is due to the unusual development of these processes. Here they afford attachment to the ligamentous cords that stretch to the posterior part of the creature's huge head.

Passing from vertebra to vertebra, and more

especially attached to the processes of the vertebræ,
are ligamentous membranes that keep the conjoined
parts in place and the spinal stem at its proper degree of curvature. Some of the ligaments—those
with the fibres going up and down, for instance—

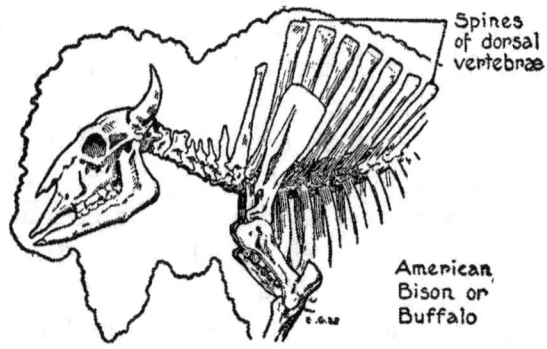

The long spines of the dorsal vertebræ of the bison, or American buffalo, give
attachments to ligaments and muscles that hold up the head.

are very elastic, and act like a spring in helping to
bring the column back to its normal position after
it has been bent. Placed between the different
vertebræ are fibrous cushions called intervertebral
disks. It is to the peculiar construction of these
cushions, found as they are between the bodies of
the vertebræ, and to the elastic quality of the sub-
stance of which they are composed, that some of
the flexibility and movement of the back-bone is
due.

Movements of the Spinal Column

The degree of movement possible in the back-bone varies. In some regions it is very limited, as, for example, in the dorsal from the third to the sixth vertebræ. This is the most unyielding part of the

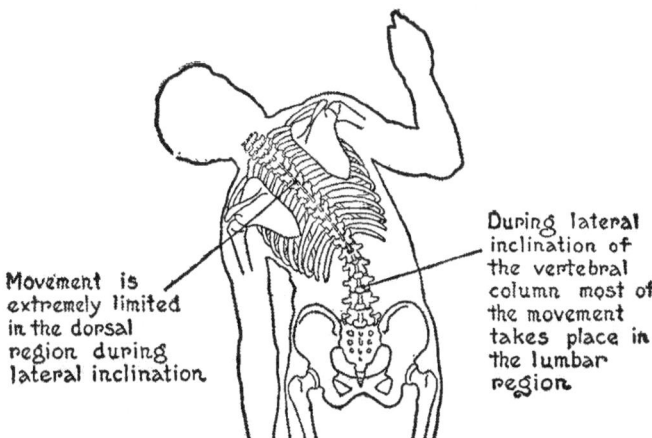

Movement is extremely limited in the dorsal region during lateral inclination.

During lateral inclination of the vertebral column most of the movement takes place in the lumbar region.

LATERAL MOVEMENTS OF THE SPINAL COLUMN.

spinal column. The lower dorsal segments, however, permit some movement in bending forward—flexion; and also in the opposite direction—extension. But between the dorsal vertebræ very little change takes place in the relative positions during lateral bending.

Most bending of the trunk, when it leans to the one side or the other, takes place in the lumbar re-

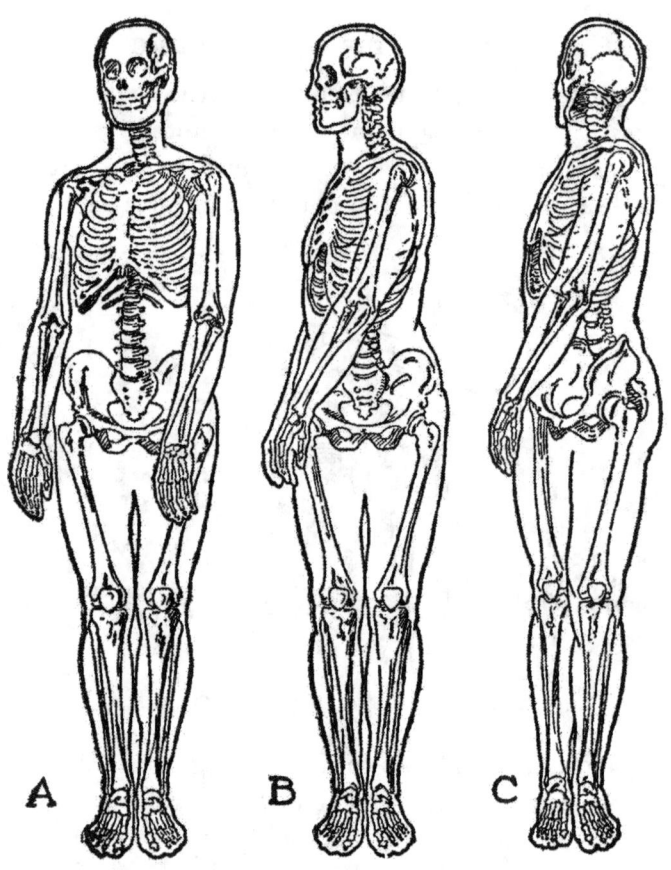

A and *B*. Rotation of the trunk.

C. The action is continued by movement in the bones of the pelvic region.

gion. Here also in bending forward, as in bowing, the movement is very free.

The back-bone can, too, in a sort of way, be rotated. This is accomplished by a twisting between some of the vertebræ. But there is very little of this movement between adjoining vertebræ on account of the particular way in which the articular surfaces fit into each other. The sum, though, of all the little changes between the segments of the whole spinal column gives a considerable degree of torsion.

When the column is thus forcibly twisted we may call it an axial rotation of the trunk. If with this movement we combine a turning of the head, it is possible to direct our eyes straight backward. By further torsion, forcibly and strongly, we are able to describe with the glance of the eye nearly three-fourths of a circle.

THE THORAX—THE RIBS AND COSTAL CARTILAGES—THE STERNUM

In general construction, the skeleton of the chest, or thorax, can be likened to a cone-shaped basket turned over, that is to say, with the apex above and the opening downward. It is formed of the twelve pairs of ribs bound posteriorly to the dorsal vertebræ, and anteriorly connected with the breast-bone. The ribs are not joined directly, however, to the breast-bone; but are connected through the intermediary of gristly parts called costal cartilages.

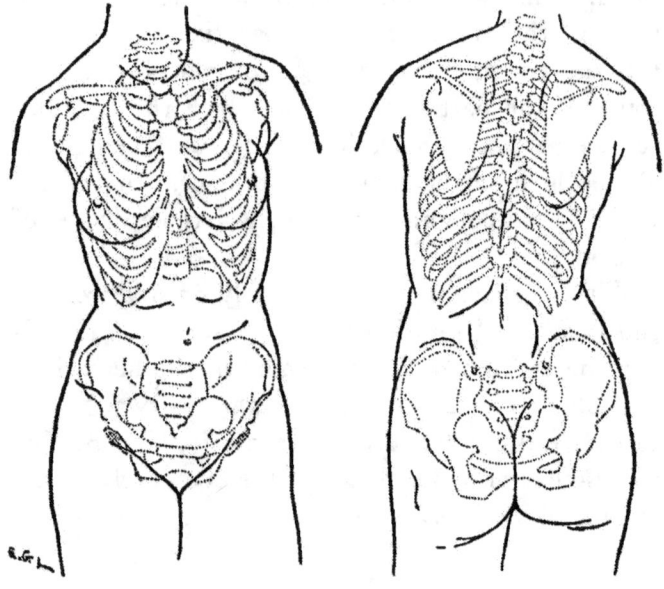

The thoracic skeleton and the pelvis give good leading lines in the preliminary constructive work in figure-drawing.

At the back the ribs are fastened to the vertebræ by joints that permit the movement necessary in the raising and lowering of the ribs in breathing.

Although in drawing from the model, it is usual, when beginning the work, to regard the thorax as a sort of fixed form so as to simplify matters, it is

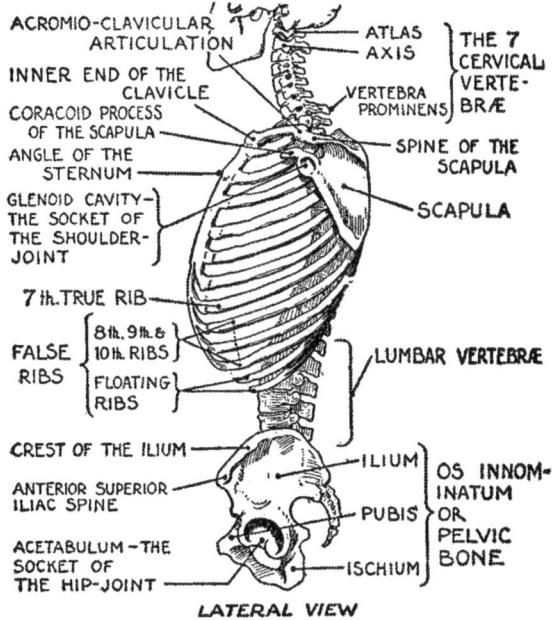

ACROMIO-CLAVICULAR ARTICULATION

INNER END OF THE CLAVICLE

CORACOID PROCESS OF THE SCAPULA

ANGLE OF THE STERNUM

GLENOID CAVITY—THE SOCKET OF THE SHOULDER-JOINT

7 th. TRUE RIB

FALSE RIBS { 8th. 9th. & 10th. RIBS } { FLOATING RIBS }

CREST OF THE ILIUM

ANTERIOR SUPERIOR ILIAC SPINE

ACETABULUM –THE SOCKET OF THE HIP-JOINT

ATLAS
AXIS
} THE 7 CERVICAL VERTE-BRÆ

VERTEBRA PROMINENS

SPINE OF THE SCAPULA

SCAPULA

LUMBAR VERTEBRÆ

ILIUM
PUBIS
ISCHIUM
} OS INNOMINATUM OR PELVIC BONE

LATERAL VIEW

THE SKELETON OF THE TRUNK.

well to keep in mind that there is some movement in the ribs. The movement is limited, however, and the general shape of the cage-like thoracic skeleton does not change very much.

As for the form of a typical rib, without particularizing too much, we may describe it as curved with a sort of sinuous twisting to this curving. Besides this particular an important characteristic is the angle in the rib near its posterior extremity.

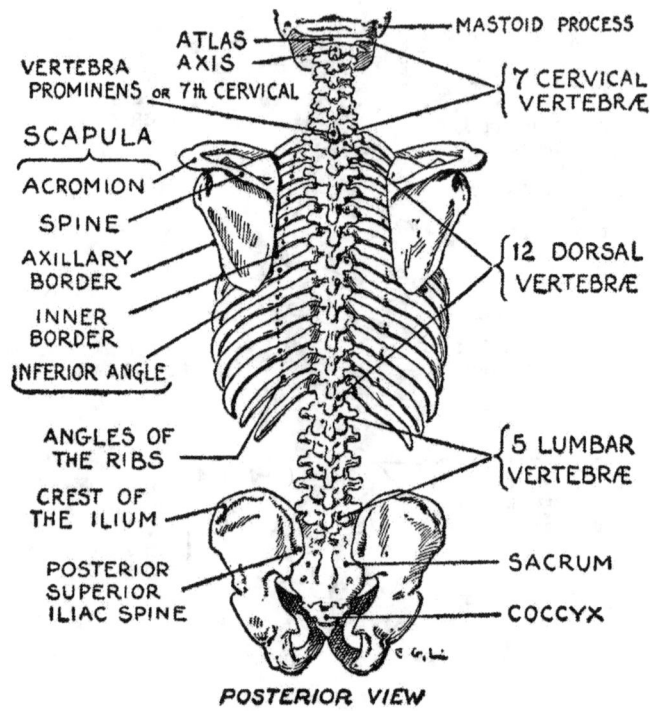

ATLAS

AXIS

VERTEBRA PROMINENS or 7th CERVICAL

MASTOID PROCESS

7 CERVICAL VERTEBRÆ

SCAPULA

ACROMION

SPINE

AXILLARY BORDER

INNER BORDER

INFERIOR ANGLE

12 DORSAL VERTEBRÆ

ANGLES OF THE RIBS

CREST OF THE ILIUM

POSTERIOR SUPERIOR ILIAC SPINE

5 LUMBAR VERTEBRÆ

SACRUM

COCCYX

POSTERIOR VIEW

THE SKELETON OF THE TRUNK.

It is the line formed by these angles of the ribs—
from the second to the eleventh, inclusive—that
marks the outer limit of a groove on the back of the
thoracic cage, the inner limit of which is the line of
the spines of the dorsal vertebræ. This is a note-
worthy particular to observe in the formation of
the posterior region of the thoracic skeleton. In

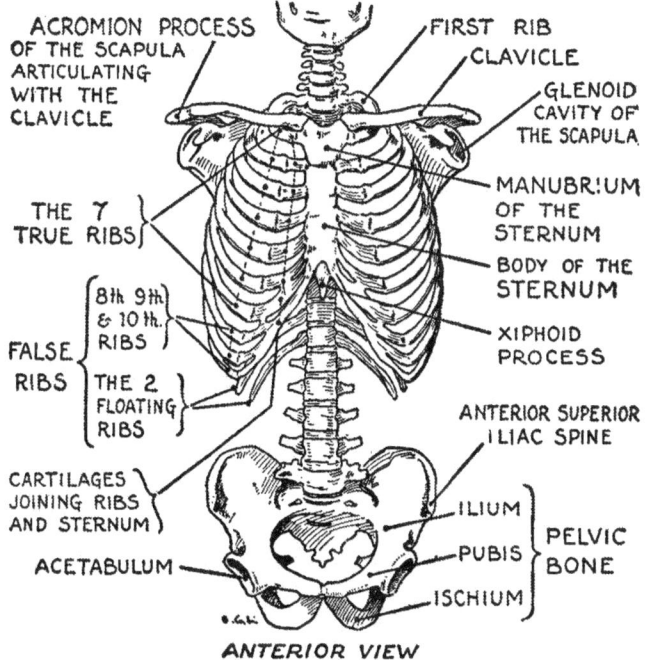

ACROMION PROCESS
OF THE SCAPULA
ARTICULATING
WITH THE
CLAVICLE

FIRST RIB
CLAVICLE
GLENOID
CAVITY OF
THE SCAPULA

THE 7
TRUE RIBS

MANUBRIUM
OF THE
STERNUM
BODY OF THE
STERNUM

8th 9th
& 10th.
RIBS
FALSE
RIBS
THE 2
FLOATING
RIBS

XIPHOID
PROCESS

ANTERIOR SUPERIOR
ILIAC SPINE

CARTILAGES
JOINING RIBS
AND STERNUM
ACETABULUM

ILIUM
PUBIS
ISCHIUM

PELVIC
BONE

ANTERIOR VIEW

THE SKELETON OF THE TRUNK.

the two grooves of each side, separated by the common median dividing line of the vertebral spines, lie portions of important muscular masses that hold the trunk upright.

Only seven of the twelve ribs—having in mind now but one side of the thorax—are connected to the breast-bone by their own individual costal cartilages. These are called true, or sternal, ribs. The remaining five are designated as false ribs; of which the two lowest are further distinguished as floating ribs. The first three false ribs—the eighth, ninth, and tenth—are joined by cartilaginous extensions to the costal cartilage of the last true rib. The line formed by this cartilaginous part—that just noted as joining some lower ribs—shows as a prominent border on the external surface. The borders of the two sides taken together mark the division between the chest and the abdomen. It is called the costal, or thoracic, arch, and it is conspicuously in evidence when the chest is raised during inspiration or in an emaciated model.

The breast-bone, the centre piece on the median line of the chest that receives the insertions of the costal cartilages, is also called the sternum. It consists of three portions; the first a short bone, extends as far as the level of the second rib. The second, or long portion, is the principal part, or body, of the bone. The third portion is but a small section, very variable in form, called the xiphoid process. This xiphoid process, also termed the ensiform appendage, has little influence on the outer form, as it is generally bent inward. Then it marks a depression in the centre of the costal arch that is known as the epigastric fossa, or the pit of the stomach.

From the xiphoid process a cord of tendinous

tissue begins, called the linea alba, that goes to the lower region of the abdomen. It will be noted in the chapter on the muscles of the trunk.

The upper or short piece of the sternum is called the manubrium, or handle; while the second sword-like body is the gladiolus. These terms, with those for the terminating section, have allusion to certain sword-like resemblances in the parts. The artist, however, had best be content with the designation of sternum, as a memory aid, in fixing this anatomical feature in his mind. The line of the sternum is that which concerns him, for it forms a very significant landmark—it marks the floor of the furrow on the chest that divides the two breast muscles. The particular view that the sternum presents to the eye is an important determining factor in starting and proceeding with a drawing. Viewed from the front, it is vertical when the model is equipoised, and from the side its direction, coming from below, goes obliquely toward the throat. But this latter line is not straight as there is a characteristic angle at the juncture of the short piece and the body of the bone. The sternum here forms a noticeable prominence called the angle of the sternum. In the model, when posed under a strong light, this angle often catches a conspicuous plane of light. The angle of the sternum, it always should be remembered, exactly marks the level of a line corresponding to the articulations of the second ribs with the sternum.

The Pelvic Bones—The Sacrum and Coccyx

The skeletal frame of the lower part of the trunk is the pelvis. This consists of the two hip-bones and the sacrum. On account of its basin-like formation, it is also called the pelvic basin. The two hip-bones are joined in front by the pubic symphysis, a nearly fixed articulation, and at the back by the intervening sacrum, which, acting like a keystone, holds the two hip-bones together.

Each half of the pelvic basin, besides the term of hip-bone, which we have so far used, is also known as the innominate bone (*os innominatum*). It can again be termed the haunch-bone, or the pelvic bone; but we will endeavor, however, for the sake of clearness throughout the book, to adhere to this latter term of pelvic bone. It is a difficult osseous formation to describe with its complexity of curving edges and the indeterminate mould of its broad parts. The three portions of which it is composed, the ilium, pubis, and ischium, are in the early life of the individual separate bones, but in the adult become united into one pelvic bone. The place where the three divisions meet is the centre of the acetabulum, or the socket of the hip-joint. The ilium, or iliac portion, as it will be referred to at times, is the largest of the three. It is irregularly wing-shaped. The upper margin of this wing, called the crest, forms laterally on the trunk the dividing line between the flank and the hip. In some cases its line

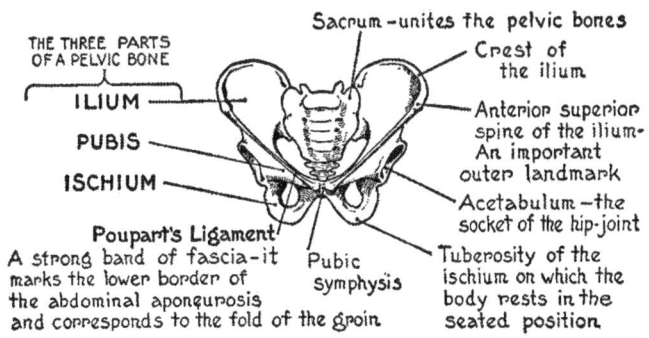

Sacrum –unites the pelvic bones

THE THREE PARTS OF A PELVIC BONE

Crest of the ilium

ILIUM

Anterior superior spine of the ilium– An important outer landmark

PUBIS

ISCHIUM

Acetabulum –the socket of the hip-joint

Poupart's Ligament
A strong band of fascia–it marks the lower border of the abdominal aponeurosis and corresponds to the fold of the groin

Pubic Symphysis

Tuberosity of the ischium on which the body rests in the seated position

THE PELVIS AND ITS DIVISIONS.

can be distinguished on the model. For the most part, though, it is masked by an overlapping border of muscle. The anterior tip, or end, of the crest is called the anterior superior iliac spine, a point that marks the beginning of the fold of the groin. The groin itself, as it passes downward and inward, corresponds to a ligament that stretches from this iliac spine to a place on the pubic bone close to the symphysis. This anatomical detail is called Poupart's ligament.

Marking a line, when drawing from life, from one anterior iliac spine to the corresponding one of the other side, is a good way of indicating the slope or slant of the hips.

A depression marks the position of this anterior superior iliac spine in a well-nourished model.

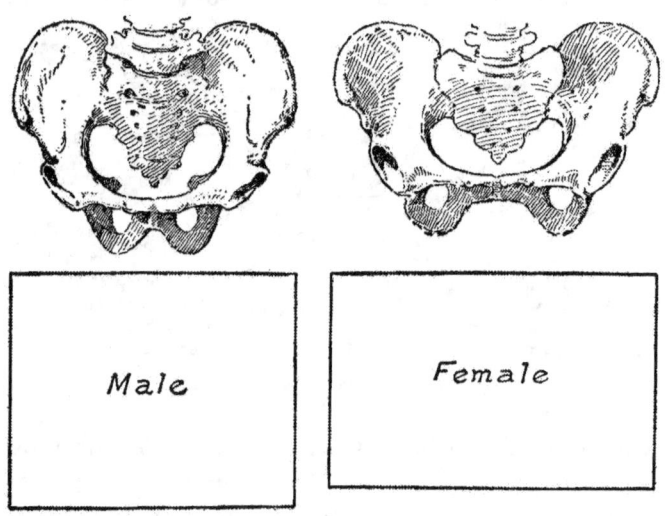

Male

Female

THE PELVIS IN THE TWO SEXES COMPARED.

The pubis, or pubic portion, forms a lower and front portion of the pelvic bone; while the ischium, or ischial portion, is the very lowest. This latter portion is characterized by a projection called the ischial tuberosity. It is on this part of the pelvis that the body rests in the seated position.

The disparity in size and the relative proportions of the middle region of the figure in the two sexes

is due to the differences in the shapes and proportions of the male and the female pelvic bones. The
female pelvis is broad and shallow; in a front view,
its outline could be enclosed within an oblong.
Relatively deeper is the male pelvis; for a right-
angled form enclosing it, viewed anteriorly, would
be nearly square. Viewed sidewise, the male pelvis
slants slightly backward, while the female inclines
forward.

The sacrum, adverted to above as holding, like
a keystone, the hip-bones together to form the
pelvic basin, is a large wedge of bone, formed of
five primitive vertebræ. The vestiges of this fact
are in the points of bone—answering to the vertebral spines—that form a crest on the posterior surface.

The coccyx, of four (usually) rudimentary segments, somewhat vertebral in formation, terminates the spinal column.

III

THE CRANIAL SKELETON

(CONTINUING THE AXIAL SKELETON)

THE IMPORTANT BONES OF THE CRANIUM

EXCEPTING the lower jaw, the skeleton of the head constitutes one formation of variously shaped bones joined by immovable articulations called sutures. The lower jaw is hinged to the skull by movable articulations.

The bones of the head can be grouped into those of the cranium and those of the face.

The cranium is composed of eight bones. Of these we will note in our study the occipital, the two parietals, the two temporals, and the frontal. The two other bony sections, the sphenoid and the ethmoid, do not come within the scope of our work as they form part of the internal region of the head. It might be well, though, to mention that the sphenoid takes an important part in the formation of the cranium. It is in such a position at the base of the skull that it acts like a keystone in binding the cranial and some of the facial bones together.

36

The occipital bone is at the back part of the cranium where the head rests on the top of the spinal column. In it is found the opening, foramen magnum, through which the beginning of the spinal cord passes. On each side of this opening are the smooth-surfaced condyles that articulate with corresponding surfaces of the atlas vertebra. It is by this articulation that the head rocks, as it were, forward and backward, and to a slight degree from side to side. On the median line in the back of the head can be felt the occipital protuberance, a strongly marked eminence to which the ligamentum nuchæ, or ligament of the nape, is attached. This ligament, which will be referred to again in the study of the musculature of this, the nuchal region, finds its points of origin on the spinous processes of some of the vertebræ.

On the examination of a skull you will notice, besides this protuberance, in this posterior region on the occipital bone, certain rough lines and surfaces. They are the places to which some of the neck and back muscles are attached. The trapezius, for instance, a very large muscle of the back, has an attachment to one of these lines.

The two parietal bones, placed immediately before the occipital, take part in the formation of the cranium at its greatest width. This, somewhat toward the back of the head, is a matter that should be especially marked for observation by the artist. A view of a skull from above will show this clearly. Each parietal bone has on its outer side a prominence called the parietal eminence, and these prominences determine this widest part of the

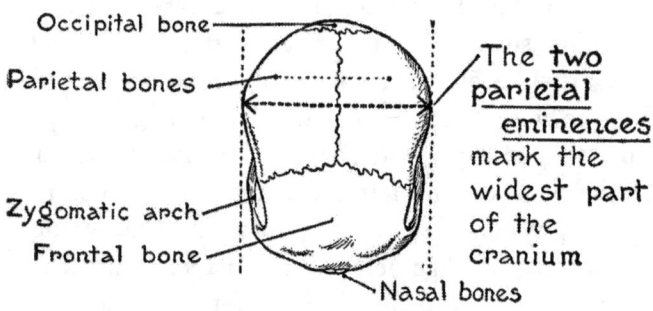

Occipital bone
Parietal bones
Zygomatic arch
Frontal bone
Nasal bones

The two parietal eminences mark the widest part of the cranium

THE SKULL VIEWED FROM ABOVE.

cranium. The parietal eminences are often observable in a subject devoid of hair in this particular region.

The frontal bone is placed immediately before the two parietals. Its principal part forms the forehead. The bone is of exceptional interest to the artist, its peculiarities are generally in evidence as they occur in places not usually hidden by hair. The frontal bone extends from the root of the nose to the crown of the head, and laterally to the edges of the forehead and the sides of the temples. In these regions the bone has significant prominences that have a great share in the formation of facial character.

First is the temporal curved line on the side of the bone; it is a continuation of a similar line that starts from the eminence of the parietal bone. This

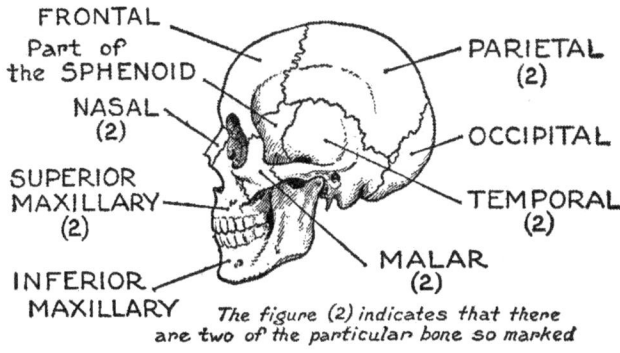

FRONTAL

Part of the SPHENOID

NASAL (2)

SUPERIOR MAXILLARY (2)

INFERIOR MAXILLARY

PARIETAL (2)

OCCIPITAL

TEMPORAL (2)

MALAR (2)

The figure (2) indicates that there are two of the particular bone so marked

THE IMPORTANT BONES OF THE HEAD.

line, as it proceeds forward, proceeds to the side of the forehead, where it forms the external angular process of the frontal bone. It forms the boundary-line between the forehead and the temple. On some heads it marks a decided angularity in the region.

Immediately above the eye on the frontal bone is a bulging out called the superciliary ridge. Often it is not present, and its degree of elevation, too, varies according to the individual. These ridges, one on each side of the forehead, should be noted in any observations and study for character. The superciliary ridges are placed, generally, but a short distance above the upper margins of the orbits, or the cavities for the eyes.

Above the root of the nose, on the frontal bone, is a space where there is sometimes a bony elevation called the nasal eminence. When the superciliary ridges are excessively developed there is a depression at this place rather than an elevation.

On each side at the upper part of the forehead is a strong character-determining elevation termed the frontal eminence. These frontal eminences when conspicuously developed in adults give the forehead a character quite anomalous and strange. The forehead is primitively composed of two frontal bones, and these frontal eminences correspond to the centres from which the bones began to harden or ossify. When in early childhood the bones have completed their ossification as one frontal bone, these centres still remain, for a time, as well-marked elevations. They are characteristic of a child's forehead, and in drawing from such models the correct delineation of their bulging goes a great way toward the success of such picturing.

The temporal bone is placed on the lateral wall of the head around the region of the ear. It sends out a process immediately in front of the ear that joins a similar process of the cheek-bone. The bridge of bone that these two processes make is an important

bony structure of the face—the zygomatic arch.
In the temporal bone is found, as can be learned on
the examination of a skull, the opening to the internal ear. Back of this opening you will observe
a large, cone-shaped protuberance. This is the

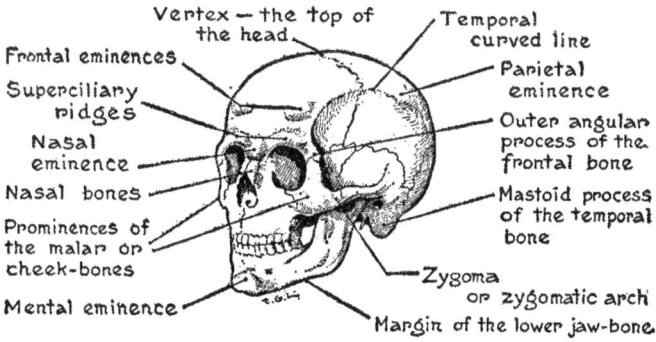

Vertex — the top of the head.
Frontal eminences
Superciliary ridges
Nasal eminence
Nasal bones
Prominences of the malar or cheek-bones
Mental eminence
Temporal curved line
Parietal eminence
Outer angular process of the frontal bone
Mastoid process of the temporal bone
Zygoma or zygomatic arch
Margin of the lower jaw-bone

PARTS OF THE SKELETON OF THE HEAD THAT INFLUENCE THE
OUTER RELIEF.

mastoid process of the temporal bone, a feature of
the skeleton of the head frequently noticeable in
the model. It can be observed back of the concha
—the shell—of the external ear. That conspicuous
cord-like muscle, which you can see coming from
the top of the sternum and passing obliquely upward across the neck, finds attachment to this
process of the temporal bone. Particulars with respect to this muscle will be found in the chapter on
the muscles of the head and neck.

On the temporal bone, under the root of the zygo-

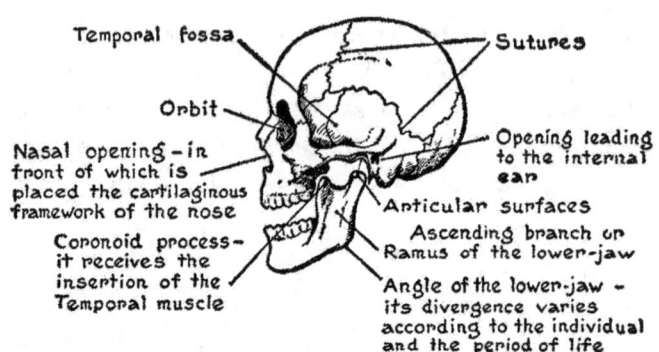

Temporal fossa

Sutures

Orbit

Nasal opening - in front of which is placed the cartilaginous framework of the nose

Coronoid process - it receives the insertion of the Temporal muscle

Opening leading to the internal ear

Articular surfaces

Ascending branch or Ramus of the lower-jaw

Angle of the lower-jaw - its divergence varies according to the individual and the period of life

VARIOUS DETAILS OF THE SKELETON OF THE HEAD.

matic process, and directly in front of the opening to the internal ear, is the place where the lower jaw hinges.

The Bones of the Face

Of the fourteen bones of the face only seven claim our attention. They are the malar, superior maxillary, and nasal, which are in pairs; and the single lower jaw-bone.

The malar, or cheek-bone, forming the prominence of the region of the cheek, is the first bone of the face that we consider.

The zygomatic arch, to which we directed our attention above, is formed by a process of the temporal, and another from a malar bone. This arch as it passes from the region of the ear to the cheek clearly shows its bony character in thin faces. Especially so in those advanced in years where the integument is dry and tensely stretched over the bones. And again in the matter of character, the malar bone plays a conspicuous part in the anatomy of the face. The significance of race depends upon its development, whether large or limited. Not forgetting in this respect, too, its position on the face, nor the breadth of the face fixed by the two malar bones.

It is only in the chubby-faced young, or the extremely plump-faced adult, that the external indications of the malar bones are not evident. A malar bone has three processes that unite with other bones. One we have already noted; namely, that taking part in forming the zygomatic arch. Another is a process that joins the outer angle of the frontal bone, and which continues the line of this angle on the side of the forehead. A third process is that joining the superior maxillary bone.

The two superior maxillary, or upper jaw-bones, form by their upper borders and with adjacent parts of the malar bones, the inferior and outer margins of the cavities for the eyes. The upper jaw-bones have their share, to be sure, in character formation, yet they do not make their form so very apparent outwardly, as their surfaces are masked by layers of facial muscles.

The two nasal bones are small osseous parts that correspond to the bridge, or ridge, of the nose. The space in front of the opening that we observe in a skull directly below the nasal bones is filled out in life by the cartilaginous framework of the nose. Although this structure gives form to the principal portion of the organ, the general mould of the nose is established by the character of the nasal bones. Their size, shape, and angle at which they are set with respect to the other bones, determine the form of the cartilaginous part as we see it in the living model. One could fairly imagine, in viewing a skull, the type of nose from the peculiarities of the nasal bones.

The inferior maxillary bone, mandible, or simply the lower jaw-bone, was in its rudimentary state composed of two bones joining at the middle of the chin. In the completely united single bone this median line of joining is termed the symphysis.

Roughly described, the lower jaw is horseshoe in shape, with the extremities ending in branches, or rami, that ascend and carry on their top condyles that fit into articular depressions of the temporal bones. This hinging of the lower jaw with the skull is by a joint permitting a threefold function. The jaw moves (1) from side to side, (2) forward and backward, and (3) the simple hinge movement of up and down, as in opening and closing the mouth. The combined articular action taking place at this joint is necessary for the seizing of the food and the grinding of it by the back teeth.

The lower border of the inferior maxillary bone is the significant line that outlines the lower part of the face—unless the subject has a mass of adipose tissue in this region completely obliterating the definition between face and throat. In respect to size, massive or small, the lower jaw has a direct bearing on the physiognomy; and its effect in the manner in which it is set with reference to the facial angle has a large share in fixing the type or character. Another matter, furthermore, that should not be overlooked by the student of faces is the degree of the angle that the lower margin of the bone makes with the margin of the ascending ramus. Often there is no angle at all, but a gradual curvature from the chin to the region of the ear. But there is, in other cases, a decided squareness at this angle.

In the region of the chin on the middle line, in the average subject, there is a slight elevation of the bone called the mental eminence, or protuberance, the word "mental" in this case having to do with the chin (Latin, *mentum*, the chin).

As the remaining seven facial bones take part in the formation of the inner skeleton of the head, they do not come within the range of our study. One, however, might be mentioned as it is observable on a skull within the orbit at its lower inner part. It is the lachrymal, a very small osseous section.

IV

THE SKELETON OF THE UPPER LIMB

The Clavicle and the Scapula (the Shoulder Girdle)

THERE are thirty-two bones in an upper limb. This includes the collar-bone and the shoulder-blade.

Now the first thing that comes under our notice in the study of the skeleton of this limb is the way in which it is joined to the rest of the bony framework. Although we see outwardly the muscular mass of the shoulder and the scapular region so compactly forming part of the general bulk of the trunk, there is in the skeleton but one point of union between the two divisions, namely, at the lower part of the throat where the collar-bone joins the sternum.

This joining is called the sternoclavicular articulation. The collar-bone, or clavicle, extends from this articulation to the summit of the shoulder. It presents to our eyes as we see it from a front view a straight line. But when looked at from above it is an elongated S-curve. Usually its formation is clearly discernible under the skin. There is, in the interval at the lower part of the throat between the two articulations of the clavicles to the top of the sternum, a depression called the pit of the neck, or the fonticulus. It is well marked, unless, as is

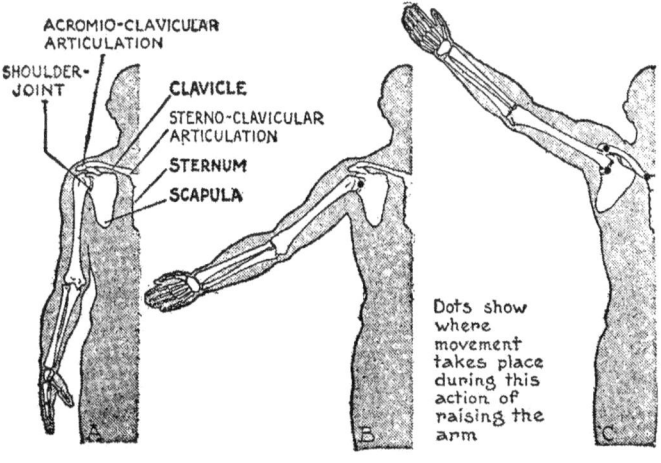

WHERE ARTICULAR MOVEMENTS TAKE PLACE IN THE SHOULDER
GIRDLE WHEN THE ARM IS RAISED.

sometimes the case in the female model, fatty tissue fills it out and makes it but slightly noticeable. Layers of fat also may mask the form of the clavicle.

In males the typical direction of the two clavicles is that of a straight line across the top of the chest. But in muscular subjects the outer clavicle ends are likely to be higher than the inner ones, while in those not strongly built the outer ends are generally the lowest.

At its outer extremity the clavicle is connected to the shoulder-blade or, as it is variously named, the blade-bone, the omoplate, or the scapula. In the course of our study we will hold to the latter term of scapula. The place where the two bones join—the acromioclavicular articulation—marks the summit of the shoulder. Here, at this joint, the kind of movement permitted is a gliding one. In this respect it is like the sternoclavicular articulation; as in both places the bones, although firmly held by their proper ligaments, glide on each other when the shoulder is raised and lowered, or thrust forward and backward.

The scapula is a flat bone, roughly triangular in outline, with a ridge, or keel, running obliquely across the upper part of its posterior surface. One angle of this triangular form—the one toward the armpit—has an expanded portion with a shallow depression that receives the globular end of the upper-arm bone. This depression is called the glenoid cavity. It is the socket of the shoulder-joint.

Practically, for our purposes, this is all the description that need be given of the scapula. The borders and angles have their special names, to

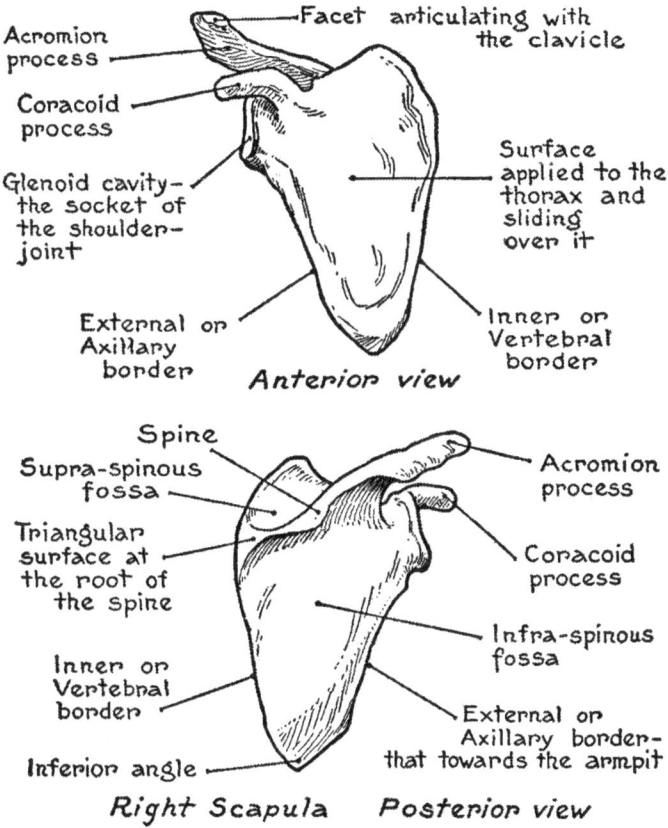

Acromion process
Coracoid process
Glenoid cavity—the socket of the shoulder-joint
External or Axillary border
Facet articulating with the clavicle
Surface applied to the thorax and sliding over it
Inner or Vertebral border

Anterior view

Spine
Supra-spinous fossa
Triangular surface at the root of the spine
Inner or Vertebral border
Inferior angle
Acromion process
Coracoid process
Infra-spinous fossa
External or Axillary border—that towards the armpit

Right Scapula   Posterior view

THE SCAPULA AND ITS PARTS.

be sure, but the terms are self-explanatory. The keel on the back is called the spine, and its edge coming close under the integument occasions a surface characteristic of considerable importance to the artist. The muscles joining its borders swell out and mark in most cases a shallow depression along its extent. On the contrary, in spare figures with little muscular development, this spine will show as a ridge instead of a depression. The outer end of

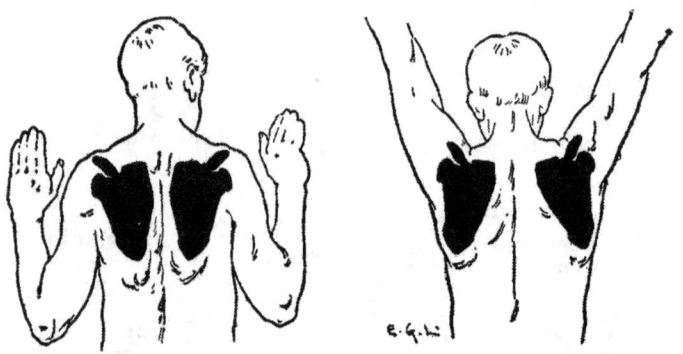

THE SCAPULÆ DURING CERTAIN MOVEMENTS OF THE SHOULDERS
AND ARMS.

the spine extends into the acromion process, to a facet on the inner margin of which an answering surface on the clavicle fits to form the articulation which we have mentioned above—the acromio-clavicular.

The inferior angle of the scapula often shows as a decided jutting out and which as it moves beneath the integument can be followed by the eye in shoulder and arm actions. The inner, or vertebral, border of the bone, that nearest the vertebral column, has a direct modification on the configuration of the back. Its movements are also observable in the various actions of the shoulder and limb. These borders of the two scapulæ, in pushing the shoulders and arms backward, approach each other very closely, while in raising the arms and thrusting them somewhat forward, the borders go very far apart.

As the acromion process at the top of the shoulder is subcutaneous, it makes, with the two clavicles, a good line to observe when drawing, especially for marking the slope of the shoulders when quickly laying in the preliminary pose of a figure.

Mention should be made here of a projection of bone on the scapula that extends beyond the rim of the glenoid cavity; named on account of its resemblance to the beak of a crow, the coracoid process. It is not subcutaneous, but is noted here as it is an important anatomical detail, three muscles finding points of attachment to its surface.

The scapula and clavicle constitute, in the terms of the naturalists, a limb-root. In the animal world, the general skeletal plan is an arrangement of a limb-root with the bones of an extremity suspended thereto. The scapula in animals is always present, and usually distinguishable throughout the different kinds by a general likeness to the triangular contour. The collar-bone, or clavicle, in some

creatures is often wanting. In the skeleton of the
horse and related beasts it is not found, and in the
cat it is represented by a splint of bone, isolated and
embedded in the muscular fibre. In these cases
and in countless other forms in the animal world the
forelimbs are not directly joined by any hard parts
to the main skeleton, but are held in place, and the
scapula kept in close contact to the thoracic walls,
by strong muscles. But in the human skeleton the
limb-root is linked to the rest of the framework by
a joining of hard parts; namely, the joint we have
referred to above, the sternoclavicular articulation.

Now the two scapulæ and the two clavicles make
up what is called the pectoral arch, or shoulder
girdle. The term girdle does not exactly fit this
formation (it is the one most employed, though),
as it is not a continuous combination of parts en-
compassing the shoulders like a girdle. There is at
the back a gap between the inner borders of the
scapulæ. In the front the formation is complete,
as the short section of the top of the sternum bridges
the gap between the two inner clavicle ends.

The examination of a mechanically articulated
skeleton in a museum, or classroom, will show the
position of this girdle in its relationship to the
thorax. By looking at the skeleton from above,
you can see how the combined formation curves

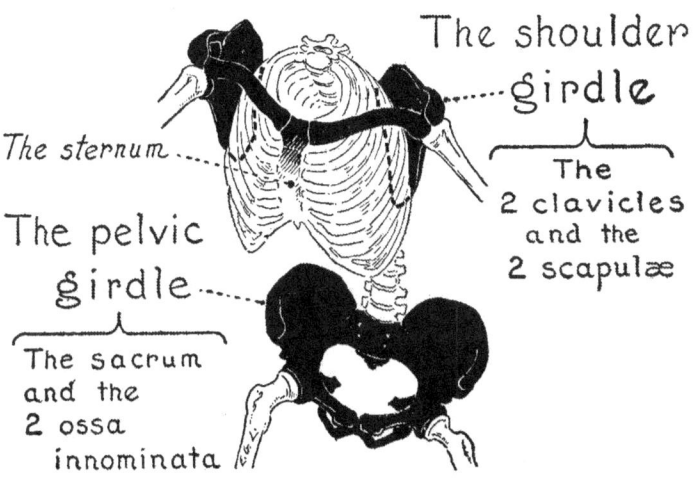

The shoulder girdle

The sternum

The 2 clavicles and the 2 scapulæ

The pelvic girdle

The sacrum and the 2 ossa innominata

THE TWO BONY GIRDLES OF THE TRUNK.

around toward the back and resting, in a way, on the cone-shaped skeleton of the thorax.

THE HUMERUS, THE RADIUS, AND THE ULNA

The upper-arm bone, or humerus, is joined to the shoulder girdle by its spherical head fitting into the glenoid cavity of the scapula, and forming the shoulder-joint. This joint, a ball-and-socket one, is strengthened and completed as such by the ligaments that surround it and other adjacent membranes that cross it. There is a great swing of movement permitted at this articulation. But rotation, which is one of these movements, and effected

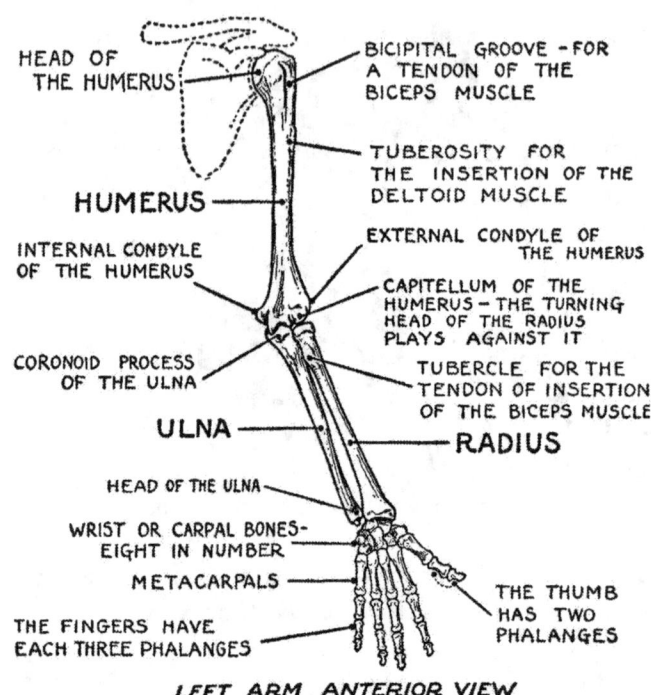

HEAD OF
THE HUMERUS

BICIPITAL GROOVE - FOR
A TENDON OF THE
BICEPS MUSCLE

TUBEROSITY FOR
THE INSERTION OF THE
DELTOID MUSCLE

HUMERUS

INTERNAL CONDYLE
OF THE HUMERUS

EXTERNAL CONDYLE OF
THE HUMERUS

CAPITELLUM OF THE
HUMERUS - THE TURNING
HEAD OF THE RADIUS
PLAYS AGAINST IT

CORONOID PROCESS
OF THE ULNA

TUBERCLE FOR THE
TENDON OF INSERTION
OF THE BICEPS MUSCLE

ULNA

RADIUS

HEAD OF THE ULNA

WRIST OR CARPAL BONES-
EIGHT IN NUMBER

METACARPALS

THE THUMB
HAS TWO
PHALANGES

THE FINGERS HAVE
EACH THREE PHALANGES

LEFT ARM ANTERIOR VIEW

THE BONES OF THE UPPER LIMB.

by the arm as a whole turning on its axis, is somewhat limited by certain strong ligaments, bony in-
terferences, and the investing fibrous capsule.

The shaft of the humerus lies pretty well in the
centre of the mass of the upper arm, the only parts
that come close enough to the surface to have any
great influence outwardly are the two projections

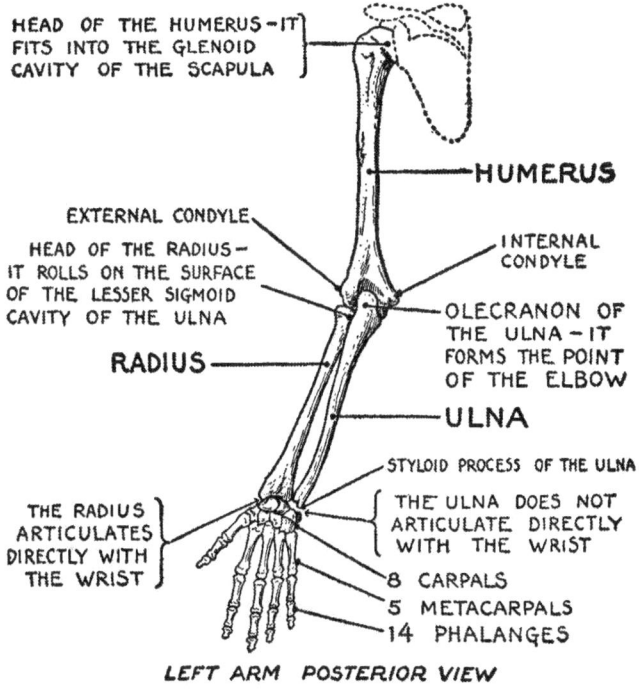

HEAD OF THE HUMERUS – IT FITS INTO THE GLENOID CAVITY OF THE SCAPULA

HUMERUS

EXTERNAL CONDYLE

HEAD OF THE RADIUS – IT ROLLS ON THE SURFACE OF THE LESSER SIGMOID CAVITY OF THE ULNA

INTERNAL CONDYLE

RADIUS

OLECRANON OF THE ULNA – IT FORMS THE POINT OF THE ELBOW

ULNA

STYLOID PROCESS OF THE ULNA

THE RADIUS ARTICULATES DIRECTLY WITH THE WRIST

THE ULNA DOES NOT ARTICULATE DIRECTLY WITH THE WRIST

8 CARPALS
5 METACARPALS
14 PHALANGES

LEFT ARM POSTERIOR VIEW

THE BONES OF THE UPPER LIMB.

at the lower end in the region of the elbow. The inner one, the internal condyle (or medial epicondyle), can be said always to be in evidence; but the outer one, the external condyle (or lateral epicondyle), is hidden by a small muscular mass when the arm is straight out. In the bent arm this external condyle forms as great a prominence as the internal one.

The bones of the forearm are two—the radius and the ulna. It will be well at this point, before we proceed with the separate consideration of these bones, to have set forth the particulars in regard to their relative positions.

When the arm is hanging by the side, in the customary position, one of the forearm bones crosses the other. Now this is not the way that they are depicted in anatomical diagrams. In these they are drawn so that the bones are parallel. This can, perhaps, be called the anatomical position, as in describing any part of the arm, the place of the item in question is named or described, with the parallel position of the two bones in mind. With the arm held so, the bones parallel, the one nearest the body (inner) is the ulna, and the one away from the body (outer) is the radius. It should be next observed that the thumb is on the same side as the radius, and that the little finger is on the side of the ulna. It will help in grasping anatomical facts of the forearm to understand fully at the start this association of outer, radial, and thumb side; and the opposite combination of inner, ulnar, and little-finger side.

Of the forearm bones the ulna only has a close joining with the humerus. The joint, that of the elbow, is hinge-like in that its play is in one plane only—forward and backward.

This hinged elbow-joint is quickly described: the end of the ulna has a deep semilunar notch that clasps a rounded surface on the opposing end of the humerus. In action the concave surface of this

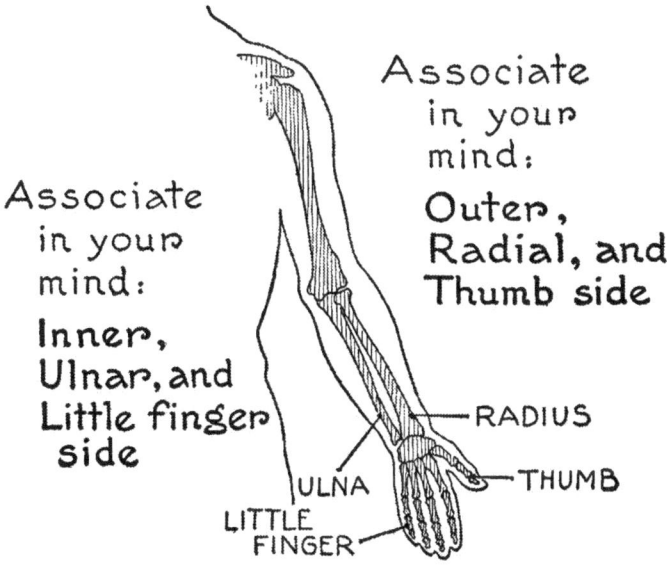

Associate in your mind:

Outer, Radial, and Thumb side

Associate in your mind:

Inner, Ulnar, and Little finger side

—RADIUS

ULNA

—THUMB

LITTLE FINGER—

A MEMORY AID IN DIAGRAMMATIC FORM.

notch, or sigmoid cavity, turns on the rounded surface, or trochlea, of the humerus.

You can notice on your own arm, by bending it back so that the hand touches the shoulder, that there are on the back of the elbow three bony prominences: the inner or medial one is the internal condyle of the humerus; the outer or lateral one the external condyle of this bone; while the middle and most protuberant, the point of the elbow, is the olecranon process of the ulna.

If now from this bent position you begin to

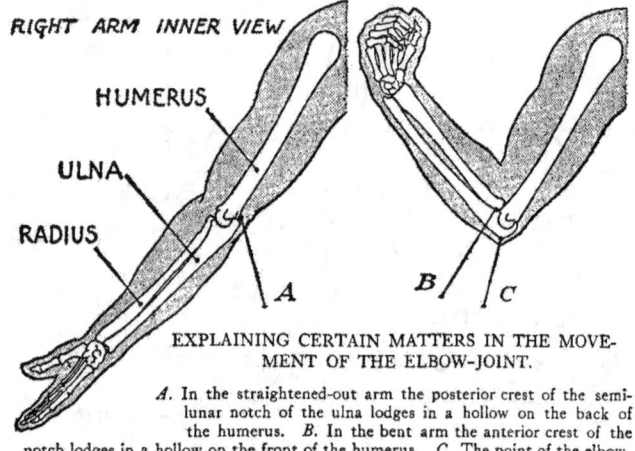

RIGHT ARM INNER VIEW

HUMERUS

ULNA

RADIUS

A *B* *C*

EXPLAINING CERTAIN MATTERS IN THE MOVE-
MENT OF THE ELBOW-JOINT.

A. In the straightened-out arm the posterior crest of the semilunar notch of the ulna lodges in a hollow on the back of
the humerus. *B.* In the bent arm the anterior crest of the
notch lodges in a hollow on the front of the humerus. *C.* The point of the elbow,
very conspicuous in the bent arm.

straighten out the arm, it will be perceived that the point of the elbow becomes less noticeable, and that when the arm is fully extended the olecranon nearly disappears. The explanation is that the crest of the semilunar notch of the ulna, forming part of the olecranon, has sunken into a hollow, the olec-ranon fossa, on the posterior surface of the hu-merus. In flexion, that is, bending the arm, a similar performance takes place on the anterior region of the elbow, in which the other crest of the semilunar notch sinks into its corresponding hollow, the coronoid fossa. As the articular parts here are covered by muscle, the action is not observable on the outer form.

Having established the identity of the prominences of the elbow, we will next consider a very important characteristic of the ulna; namely, its subcutaneous crest. From the point of the elbow—the olecranon—move the tips of the fingers of the opposite hand along the forearm toward the little finger. The fingers will have followed, if you have pressed down into the mass of the forearm, this crest of the ulna. This is an item of much meaning to the student of anatomy, as it gives a division of the two main groups of forearm muscles. This division between the muscle groups forms in the region a characteristic of the forearm called the ulnar furrow. It is a feature apparent in nearly all arms, even slightly so in plump arms.

The ulna is not a straight bone, it resembles very much an attenuated double curve, which fact can be appreciated by the little experiment suggested above of following the subcutaneous crest of the bone. The ulnar furrow leads to a knob-like eminence at the wrist, a prominence that is particularly in evidence when the forearm is in pronation, a position opposed to supination, a matter of which we will speak presently. This knob of bone is the round head of the ulna (in this case the lower end of a bone is termed the head). A pointed part of the lower end of the ulna, the styloid process, also forms, in the position of supination, a prominence observable externally.

The ulna has no direct articulation with the bones of the wrist. The radius is the bone that carries the true articulation from the forearm to the wrist-bones.

The radius, external and thumb-side bone of the forearm, is, at the wrist, of a heavy, squarish character. Its joining to the wrist-bones is close, and the contour of the forearm continues without much of a break to the wrist and hand. In thus speaking of this continuity of line we have in mind its dissimilarity to the contour of the ulnar side. Here the line coming from the forearm and passing to the hand is broken by the prominence of the ulna head and the concavities it causes, together with a slighter eminence of a wrist-bone. All this in connection with a very difficult matter of drawing in figure work—the proper placing of a hand on the forearm. There should be manifest in any such picturing a clear understanding of the anatomical structure of the region by a proper attention to the bony characteristics that show on the outer form.

The upper end of the radius, the head, is of an interesting character, both in form and function. And rather mechanistic, too, in design, for it is in fact wheel-like, and has a wheel-like motion. This radius head resembles a thick button, set on the superior extremity of the bone; the free side, or top, being concave, is adapted to the rounded surface, or capitellum, of the humerus; while the edge of the button fits into the hollow on the ulna, called the radial notch. A ring of ligament holds this head close to the articular surface of the radial notch. Adjacent ligaments of the elbow-joint keep the radius head top in contact with the capitellum of the humerus. The peculiarities of movement that take place at this articulation are as follows: the radius, when it rotates, rolls the edge of the wheel-like head in its proper articular notch in the ulna, and at the same time plays its concave top against the round capitellum of the humerus. The lower end of the radius, however, has an entirely different movement. It moves circularly over the neighboring end of the ulna. This is due to the fact that the shaft of the radius is not straight. It is slightly curved; the curvature flaring out so that while the upper end of the bone truly rotates and turns on its axis, the lower end describes an arc of a circle.

It is this structural peculiarity of the radius and

the two forms of movement just now indicated that make possible supination and pronation.

Now in the attitude of supination (the anatomical position, noted immediately above) the hand

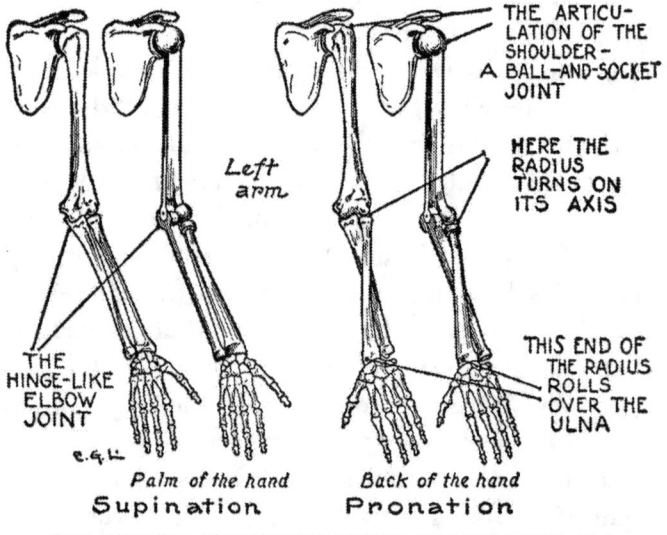

THE ARTICU-
LATION OF THE
SHOULDER—
A BALL-AND-SOCKET
JOINT

HERE THE
RADIUS
TURNS ON
ITS AXIS

Left arm

THE
HINGE-LIKE
ELBOW
JOINT

THIS END OF
THE RADIUS
ROLLS
OVER THE
ULNA

Palm of the hand
Supination

Back of the hand
Pronation

THE SKELETAL COMPONENTS OF THE ARM ARRANGED AS A MECHANISM.

is supine; that is, the palm faces upward or forward; while in pronation the hand is prone; that is, the palm has been made to face downward or backward.

These two opposing movements of the forearm and hand are like this: starting with the radius and the ulna parallel, we move the thumb forward,

begin to turn it inward and then backward, carrying with it the palm, which is at last directed to
the back.   In this act we have caused the radius
to cross in front of the ulna, and so have pronated

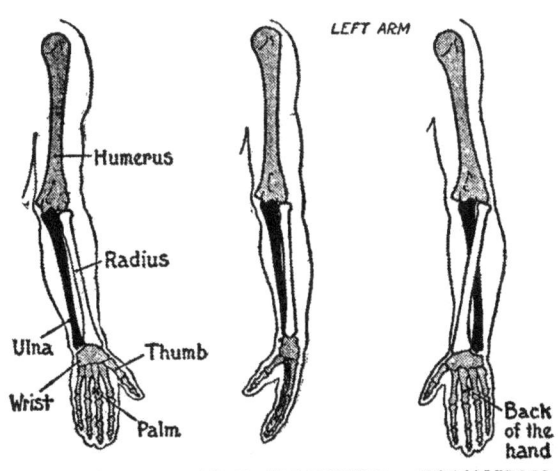

LEFT ARM

Humerus

Radius

Ulna   Thumb

Wrist

Palm

Back
of the
hand

SUPINATION   SEMI-PRONATION   PRONATION

THE ACTION OF THE RADIUS IN THESE MOVEMENTS.

the forearm.   Reverse the performance and bring
the arm back to the first position, we have supinated the forearm.

A particular that should be noted in the structural frame of the arm is this: when the arm is in
supination, the axes of the two sections of the arm
make, viewed anteriorly, an obtuse angle at the
elbow; but when the arm is in pronation the two

axes approximately coincide; that is, the arm has practically one axis. This could be made very clear by diagrams, but it would be best to observe it in your own arm.

If you have tried this pronation and supination in your own arm you, no doubt, have noticed how the radius seemed to be the bone that carried the hand with it during these actions. This, in point of fact, is the case, for it is to the radius alone that the wrist finds its proper joining; the ulna end at the wrist does not enter in any true articular connection with the wrist-bones. A thick, fibrous cartilage interposes between it and the carpus.

THE BONES OF THE WRIST AND THE HAND

The wrist, or carpus, is composed of eight bones. Two of these only articulate with the radius; they are the scaphoid and semilunar. In the same row with these, and counting next in order from the thumb side, is the cuneiform, and then the pisiform. In the second row, again counting from the thumb, is the trapezium, the trapezoid, the os magnum, and the unciform. The scaphoid is also termed the navicular bone, and the semilunar the lunate bone. The unciform is also designated as the hooked bone.

The pisiform bone (Latin, *pisum*, pea), is but a globular osicle that is considered generally as a sesamoid bone. It is placed on the inner anterior region almost free from the other carpals, articulating only by a small facet with its contiguous bone, the cuneiform.

To our eye both surfaces of the wrist, front and

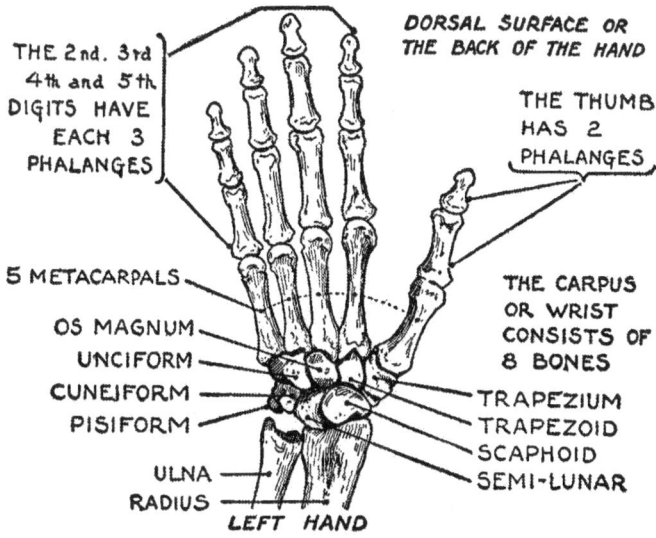

DORSAL SURFACE OR THE BACK OF THE HAND

THE 2nd. 3rd 4th and 5th DIGITS HAVE EACH 3 PHALANGES

THE THUMB HAS 2 PHALANGES

5 METACARPALS

OS MAGNUM

UNCIFORM

CUNEIFORM

PISIFORM

THE CARPUS OR WRIST CONSISTS OF 8 BONES

TRAPEZIUM

TRAPEZOID

SCAPHOID

SEMI-LUNAR

ULNA

RADIUS

LEFT HAND

THE BONES OF THE WRIST AND HAND.
(Compare with the diagram of the bones of the foot on page 85.)

back, are similarly somewhat convex. But in the skeleton, when devoid of soft parts, the carpal group of bones from the palm side shows as a hollow. This is occasioned by the general arched formation of the carpus as a whole, and also by the higher position on the one side of the pisiform and the hooked process of the unciform; and on the other side by a projecting ridge of the trapezium. This

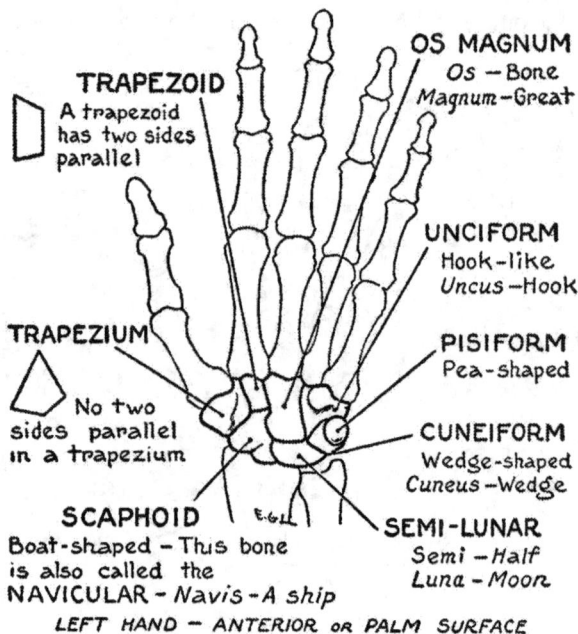

OS MAGNUM
Os — Bone
Magnum — Great

TRAPEZOID
A trapezoid
has two sides
parallel

UNCIFORM
Hook-like
Uncus — Hook

TRAPEZIUM
No two
sides parallel
in a trapezium

PISIFORM
Pea-shaped

CUNEIFORM
Wedge-shaped
Cuneus — Wedge

SCAPHOID
Boat-shaped — This bone
is also called the
NAVICULAR — *Navis — A ship*

SEMI-LUNAR
Semi — Half
Luna — Moon

LEFT HAND — ANTERIOR OR PALM SURFACE

THE CARPAL BONES AND HELPS IN REMEMBERING
THEIR NAMES.

hollow is filled up in the living subject by tendons of forearm muscles that pass here to their attachments to the different bones of the hand.

At the line of union between the two rows of carpal bones is the midcarpal articulation, where there

is considerable movement. Although numerous ligaments bind the carpal bones together, they move on
each other—the whole character of which movement can be summarized as of a gliding nature.

Next in order come the five metacarpal bones,
four of which constitute the skeleton of the body
of the hand. The remaining one is that belonging
to the thumb. This, set on the body of the hand
obliquely to the other metacarpals, forms the basic
structure of the ball of the thumb. The articulation by which this particular metacarpal is joined
to its proper carpal bone—the trapezium, is one
that permits movement in all directions but rotation. The joint is saddle-like in plan, the two bones
fitting into each other with reciprocal curves on their
articular surfaces. The peculiar arrangement permits the metacarpal to rock, as it were, on the trapezium, and so allowing that great mobility of the
human thumb. A web of integument stretches from
the thumb to the body of the hand to hold it in
place and limit the range of movement. Muscular
fibres also have their share in these matters.

The four finger metacarpals that form the structure of the body of the hand are held together rather
firmly by strong ligamentous parts. They constitute, with the thumb metacarpal, the skeleton of
the palm.

The first row of knuckles—those popularly meant

by "the knuckles," that are so prominent when the fist is clenched—are the heads of the metacarpal bones where they articulate with the first row of

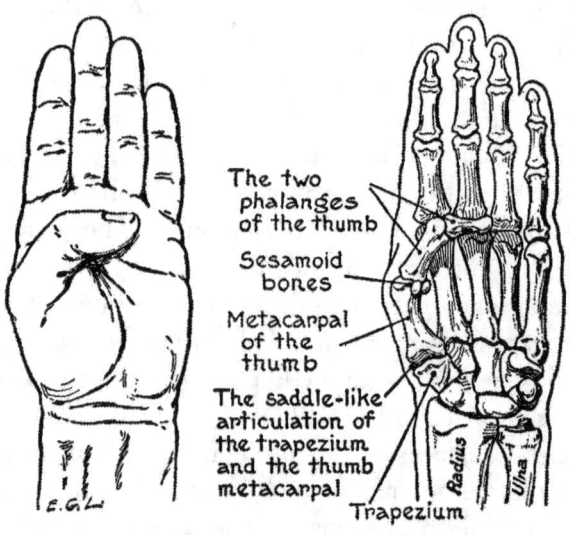

The two phalanges of the thumb

Sesamoid bones

Metacarpal of the thumb

The saddle-like articulation of the trapezium and the thumb metacarpal

Radius

Ulna

Trapezium

TO EXPLAIN THE MOVEMENT IN THE SKELETAL PART OF THE THUMB.

finger phalanges. The other knuckle-joints are between the different phalanges.

The bony segments of the fingers and the free part of the thumb are the phalanges. Each separate bone of this skeletal division is called a phalanx. There are fourteen phalanges, and as you can see with your own eyes, each finger has three, and the thumb but two. It is that row of prominent "knuckles" just alluded to that forms part of the articulations of the first row of finger phalanges to their metacarpal bones. An articulation here is of such a plan structurally that movement is possible somewhat freely in all directions but that of bending the finger back to the dorsal surface of the hand.

The corresponding joint in the thumb—that between the metacarpal and the phalanx—allows of but flexion and extension.

In the joints between the different phalanges only flexion and extension take place. Flexion is exemplified by the grasping of the fingers, and extension in straightening them out. Extension is, in a degree, checked by ligaments that prevent the fingers from bending back too far.

As it is of particular importance for an artist to know where the bony anatomy affects the outer form, we will go over in review the various regions of the shoulder and upper limb in which the osseous parts come close enough to the skin to modify or influence the outer relief:

Clavicle.—Its entire length.

Scapula.—The acromion process, its spine, vertebral border, and the inferior angle.

Humerus.—The condyles; the internal one especially.

Ulna.—The olecranon process; the crest along the ulnar furrow; the prominence of the head at the wrist.

Radius.—Its bulky square character at the wrist. (The wheel-like head of the radius can be felt in rotation if a finger is placed immediately in front of the external condyle of the humerus.)

Carpus.—In very thin hands a few wrist-bones can sometimes be identified; the pisiform at the base of the ball of the little finger, and near the base of the ball of the thumb, the scaphoid.

Hand.—On the dorsal surface, the four metacarpals are very close to the skin.

The "knuckles," the prominent joinings of the four inner metacarpals with the first row of finger phalanges. The joint belonging to the middle finger is the largest. The interphalangeal joints.

The slightly enlarged ends of the thumb bones at the articulations. Note the character of the nail-phalanx of the thumb, how it has an outward-turning direction.

V

THE SKELETON OF THE LOWER LIMB

The Pelvic Girdle

BEFORE we direct our attention to the skeletal details of the lower limb we will give a few moments' thought again to the pelvic bones and their structural design and relationship to the lower limbs. The two bones of the pelvis with their binding keystone at the back—the sacrum—constitute the lower bony encircling formation of the trunk, the pelvic girdle.

The pelvic girdle, rather firmly held together, is to be thought of by the artist as one rigid construction, as its form gives such good suggestions in establishing lines for drawing in the preliminary blocking out of a figure.

The skeleton of the lower limb swings on, or depends from, the pelvic girdle. The place where it is thus fastened is the hip-joint, where the globular head of the thigh-bone is received into the acetabulum, or socket of that joint.

The Bones of the Thigh and the Leg

A lower limb, not including the pelvis, has thirty bones in its make-up. Of these we will study first that of the thigh, the two bones of the leg, and then that of the knee; being respectively the femur, the tibia and fibula, and the patella.

The general arrangement of the bones of the lower limb is similar to that of the upper limb. This homology in the structural design of the two limbs should be particularly noticed, because, if we have learned the characteristics of the bony framework of one limb, such knowledge by analogy will help us recognize the like qualities in the structure of the other limb.

But in the inferior extremity we find an extra bone, the patella, or bone of the knee. This is considered functionally, however, a sesamoid bone; that is, it is placed so that it acts as a pulley to give greater power to a muscle, the tendon of which passes over the articulation of the knee.

The thigh-bone, or femur, is the longest bone in the body. Its round, articular head is much more spherical than the head of the humerus. The reciprocal cavity of the joint is deep; in point of fact, it is a veritable cup, while the socket of the shoulder-joint is only a shallow depression. The fitting of the answering parts in the hip articulation is a de-

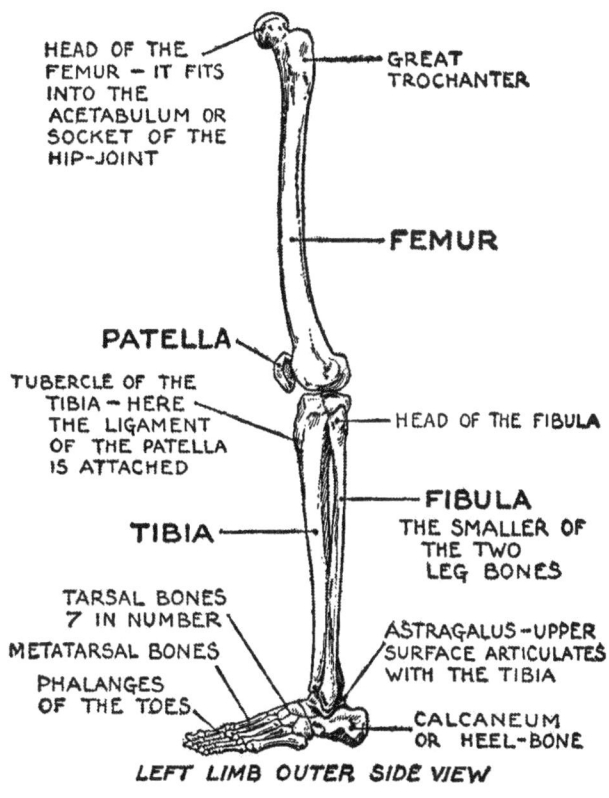

HEAD OF THE FEMUR — IT FITS INTO THE ACETABULUM OR SOCKET OF THE HIP-JOINT

GREAT TROCHANTER

FEMUR

PATELLA

TUBERCLE OF THE TIBIA — HERE THE LIGAMENT OF THE PATELLA IS ATTACHED

HEAD OF THE FIBULA

FIBULA THE SMALLER OF THE TWO LEG BONES

TIBIA

TARSAL BONES 7 IN NUMBER

METATARSAL BONES

PHALANGES OF THE TOES

ASTRAGALUS — UPPER SURFACE ARTICULATES WITH THE TIBIA

CALCANEUM OR HEEL-BONE

LEFT LIMB OUTER SIDE VIEW

THE BONES OF THE LOWER LIMB.

cidedly tight one, and it can be said to be a true ball-and-socket joint.   Now a certain supplementary variety in the range of movement possible in the hip-joint is given to the limb by the way in which

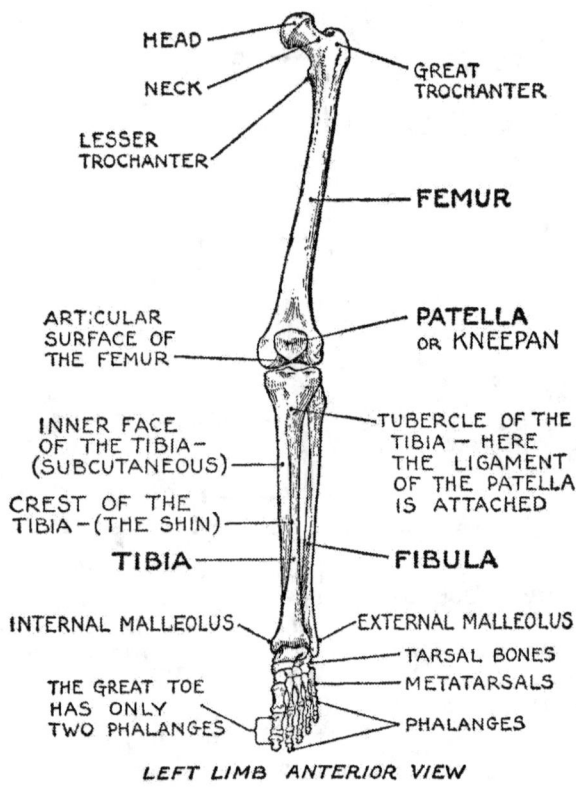

LEFT LIMB ANTERIOR VIEW

THE BONES OF THE LOWER LIMB.

the head of the femur is placed on a short section of the shaft, known as the neck, and by the fact that this neck is placed obliquely to the shaft of the bone. The degree of the angle at which this neck

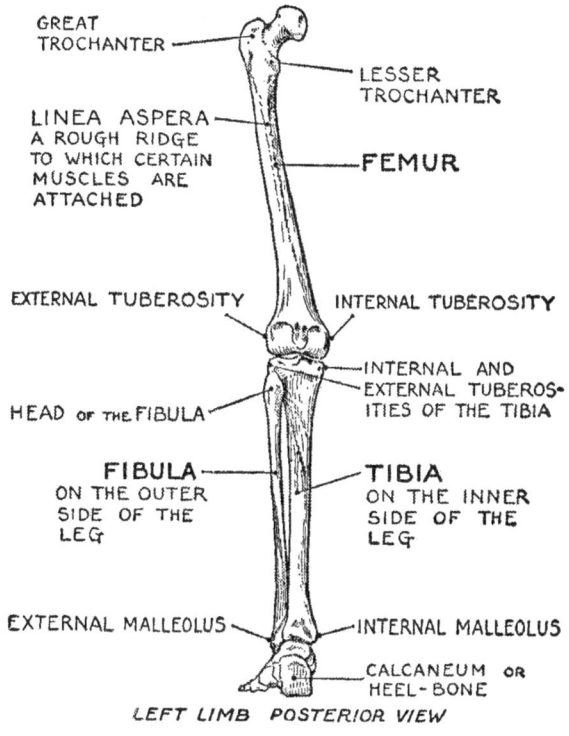

GREAT
TROCHANTER

LESSER
TROCHANTER

LINEA ASPERA
A ROUGH RIDGE
TO WHICH CERTAIN
MUSCLES ARE
ATTACHED

FEMUR

EXTERNAL TUBEROSITY

INTERNAL TUBEROSITY

INTERNAL AND
EXTERNAL TUBEROS-
ITIES OF THE TIBIA

HEAD OF THE FIBULA

FIBULA
ON THE OUTER
SIDE OF THE
LEG

TIBIA
ON THE INNER
SIDE OF THE
LEG

EXTERNAL MALLEOLUS

INTERNAL MALLEOLUS

CALCANEUM OR
HEEL-BONE

LEFT LIMB POSTERIOR VIEW

THE BONES OF THE LOWER LIMB.

is set varies in different individuals. This particular has a marked influence on the posture and
proportions in the hips of a figure.

The great trochanter of the femur is an important
item for the artist to take note of. It is a promi-

nence on the outer side of the bone externally to the
angle where the neck joins the shaft. It is a point
of attachment for some of the large muscular parts
of the region, and an outer landmark of great assis-
tance in determining the action of the figure. When
the model is standing perfectly straight with the
weight of the body equipoised on the legs, the great
trochanters of both femurs are level and mark the
widest part of that region. When the model is
standing, however, with the weight thrown on one
leg, the great trochanter of this weight-sustaining
leg is thrust out and shows as a considerable prominence. Its hard, bony surface can be felt directly
underneath the integument. On the other side of
the hips, the trochanter of the relaxed limb is not
externally apparent, as its protuberance is lost in
the soft parts of the region.

A good line to draw for marking the slope of the
hips in the average standing pose is that through
the two trochanters. The prominence of the one
on the supporting limb is easily indicated; but the
position of the one on the relaxed side must be determined and marked as well as you can. This
line would be a companion line to the one suggested
for showing the slope of the hips, and that was to
be drawn between two points on the pelvic bones,
that is, the two anterior superior iliac spines.

On the posterior border of the femur, below the

neck, toward the inner side, is another salient called the lesser trochanter. Although this is not sub-cutaneous, it is of interest to us as it is an important place of attachment for some muscular forms. It is from here that a curved line begins that merges with another curved line of the opposite side to form the rough ridge on the back of the femur known as the linea aspera. It is to this rough line that certain muscles are attached.

The lower end of the femur—at the knee—widens out on each side into projections of the bone termed respectively the external and internal tuberosities. They are also called, for the outer one, the lateral epicondyle, and for the inner one the medial epi-condyle. This lower part of the femur in the region of the tuberosities, wide and bulky, comes in con-tact by its articular surface with the next bone of the limb, the tibia, to form with it and the patella the bony system of the knee.

The tibia is the principal bone of the leg (using the word "leg" in its proper meaning for the part of the limb between the knee and the foot). It is a strong bone placed on the inner side, with the ends greatly enlarged at the knee and forming two prominences—its internal and its external tuber-osities. The lower extremity is also enlarged, but relatively not so much; its inner portion expands to form the internal, or medial, malleolus, or projec-

tion of the ankle-joint. The corresponding bony
projection on the other side of the ankle is the external, or lateral malleolus, but it is formed by the
lower end of the second bone of the leg, the fibula.

The fibula, or peroneal bone, or, as it is sometimes
named on account of its slender form, the splint-
bone, is in certain respects not structurally an important bone, as, for instance, in carrying the weight
of the body. It is the tibia articulating at the knee
with the femur that feels the force of the weight,
and it is this leg-bone that transmits the weight to
the ankle-joint, and thence to the foot.

A matter that should be clearly understood with
respect to the fibula is that it is placed on the outer
side of the leg, and again, that it is embedded for
about three-fourths of its length within the muscular mass of the region. Only its lower extremity,
the lateral malleolus and adjacent part of the shaft,
and the head on the outer region near the knee
are subcutaneous.

Now as to the articulation of the knee: for our
work we only need to think of its function as a sort
of hinge-joint, or one permitting the bending and
the straightening out of the limb, and how the patella acts as a pulley for the large muscular mass
of the front of the thigh. To describe its articular
parts, it will suffice to say that the smooth surfaces
of the ends of the tibia and femur (with thin cush-

ions of tissue between them) roll, or rock, on each other, the bones being held in contact and in their proper places by lateral ligaments, prevented from twisting in the wrong way by check ligaments, and in various ways held by other membranes, including a joint capsule and tendons of muscles.

The examination of an artificially joined skeleton will show that the bones here are not very closely fitted together. There is not in this joint that mechanistic likeness found in the joints of the hip or elbow. The knee, nevertheless, owing to the numerous ligaments and membranes that invest it, is a very strong articulation.

The patella, kneecap, or kneepan, as it is variously called, is a small bone forming the anterior prominence of the knee. It lies in front of the lower end of the femur; its apex, its lowermost point, is at the level of the line of the articulation. The patella is more or less embedded within the fibres of a large tendon that crosses the front of the knee, which tendon is itself the chief factor in keeping the bone in its place. Below the patella the tendon is given the separate name of the ligament of the patella, and it is attached to a special point on the tibia called the tubercle of the tibia.

The distance of the patella from the place where the patellar ligament is inserted is approximately the same in all movements of the knee-joint. This is due to the particular quality of the ligament, which is of a springy nature, yet does not stretch nor lengthen its fibres.

On the examination of the patella when the limb is held straight with the muscles relaxed, the bone

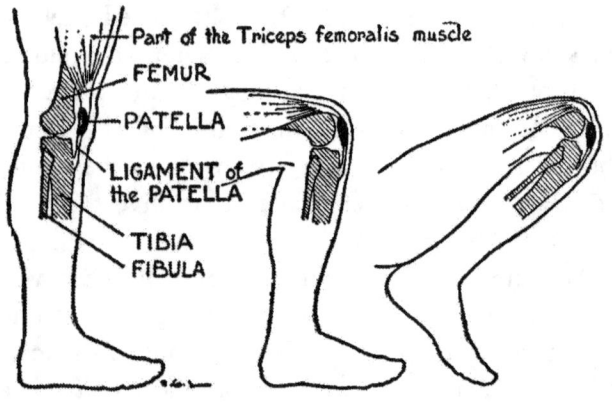

DIAGRAMMATIC REPRESENTATION OF THE MOVEMENT IN THE KNEE-JOINT.

is observed as loosely held and capable of being moved from side to side. Now, if the muscles of the limb are put into tension, either by flexion or simply straining the fibres, the patella immediately is found to become fixed and immovable.

The bony landmarks of the region of the knee during the different positions of the joint in movement are not obscure, yet they are really hard to appreciate correctly when we attempt to draw them, or represent them, in modelling. The patella form is somewhat clear in some positions, but in strong flexion, its relief becomes lost and is combined with the general roundness of the bent knee. A knowledge of the underlying bony structures helps in a better visual appreciation of the varied roundness of the region. Among the reliefs at this region are those of the internal and external tuberosities of the femur and the internal and external tuberosities of the tibia.

Even the trochlear or articular surface of the femur in some positions has an influence on the outer form. This is when the knee is bent, and the ligament of the patella holds the patella in the same relative position whether the tibia or the femur is moving, and the trochlea of the femur, which is ordinarily in contact with the articular top of the tibia, becomes, as it moves away from the patella, partly subcutaneous in front of the bent knee.

In the bent, or flexed, knee (that is, in the kneeling position), it is the patella which receives the weight of the body. A curious matter, though properly related to pathology, might be mentioned here. It is this: a little sac of lubricating fluid (prepatellar bursa), placed in front of the patella, becomes inflamed in those who are compelled, by their occupation, to be much on their bended knees; this malady is commonly called housemaid's knee.

Within the knee-joint are found pellets of fat filling out the free places. In flexion they are displaced by the other parts; for instance, the tense ligament of the patella will have, bordering it on each side, slight reliefs of these pellets. They will be of indefinite form and soft to the touch.

In addition to the patella and the other bony markings of the region of the knee, there is another landmark which we must not neglect to mention; namely, the tubercle of the tibia, where the ligament of the patella is inserted. It is an unmistakable eminence, and an important one for the artist to observe, especially when the leg is viewed in profile.

Descending from the tubercle to the inner side of the leg is the subcutaneous surface of the tibia. This is sometimes termed the shin; but, to be exact, this term had best be applied to the sharp, anterior crest of the bone. We have in the subcutaneous surface of the tibia a well-established feature for drawing. Its curvature is clearly perceived from the inner knee downward to the ankle, where it terminates on the internal malleolus. In the matter of etymology, the name malleolus is from the Latin *malleus*, a hammer or mallet; the significance of the term can be understood by picturing in the mind a tibia bone with its expanded, mallet-like end.

As we have observed, the internal malleolus represents the lower end of the tibia.   Now, the corresponding bony prominence on the outer side of the

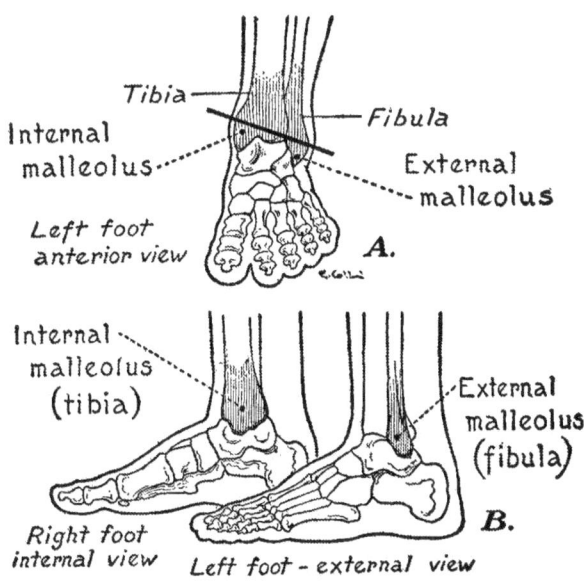

Tibia —
Internal malleolus···

— Fibula
External
··· malleolus

Left foot
anterior view   *A.*

Internal ··.
malleolus ′···.
(tibia)

·External
malleolus
(fibula)

Right foot
internal view   Left foot - external view   *B.*

TO SHOW THE RELATIVE POSITIONS OF THE PROMINENCES OF THE
ANKLE–JOINT.

A. The internal malleolus is higher than the external one   *B.* The internal malleolus is farther forward than the external one.

ankle is the external malleolus, which is formed by the lower end of the fibula.   These enlarged ends of the two leg-bones give at the ankle important landmarks for the artist to observe.   It will be a great help for him in drawing to have an unforgettable idea of the relative positions, and the different levels, at which the two malleoli are set.

First, observe again that the bulky mass of the internal, or medial, malleolus is formed by the expanded heavy end of the tibia; while the smaller, sharply defined external, or lateral, malleolus represents the end of the smaller fibula. Now, the thing that you should notice and remember is this: the internal malleolus is higher than the external one. To make the matter still clearer, always keep in mind that a line drawn as an axis of the ankle-joint, through the centres of the two malleoli, runs, from within, obliquely outward and downward. Another characteristic of the region is that the bulk of the internal malleolus is placed forward, close to the bend of the ankle, while the prominence of the external one is placed farther back, about half-way between the bend of the ankle and the heel.

THE ANKLE-BONES AND THOSE OF THE FOOT

What we call the drawing of the foot is, in general, founded on its bony framework. We have seen that the prominences of the ankle are based on the expanded lower ends of the two leg-bones; so, likewise, the back or dorsum of the foot, with the exception of one small muscular form and some tendons, is established by the skeletal parts only.

The ankle, part of the arch of the foot, and the

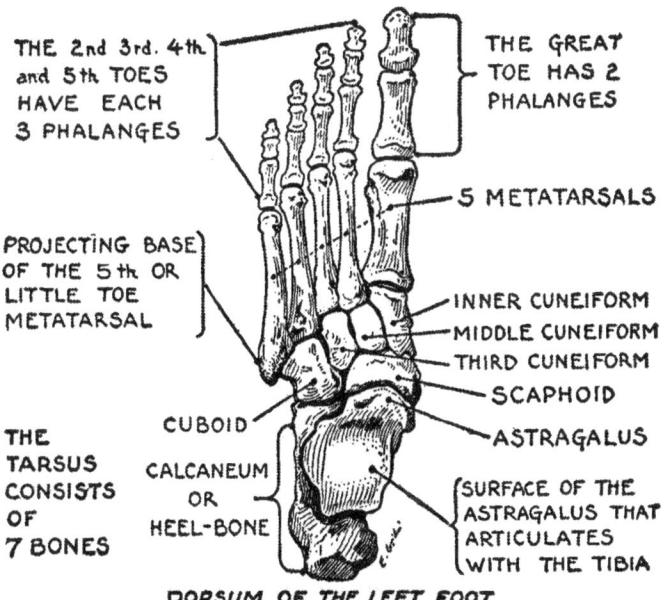

THE 2nd 3rd. 4th. and 5th TOES HAVE EACH 3 PHALANGES

THE GREAT TOE HAS 2 PHALANGES

5 METATARSALS

PROJECTING BASE OF THE 5th OR LITTLE TOE METATARSAL

INNER CUNEIFORM

MIDDLE CUNEIFORM

THIRD CUNEIFORM

SCAPHOID

CUBOID

THE TARSUS CONSISTS OF 7 BONES

CALCANEUM OR HEEL-BONE

ASTRAGALUS

SURFACE OF THE ASTRAGALUS THAT ARTICULATES WITH THE TIBIA

DORSUM OF THE LEFT FOOT

THE BONES OF THE FOOT.

(Compare with the diagram of the bones of the wrist and hand on page 65.)

heel are formed by the seven tarsal bones, which group of bones answers to the carpal bones of the upper limb. (As we remember, however, there are eight carpal bones.)

The seven bones that constitute the structure of

the tarsus are the astragalus, calcaneum, scaphoid, cuboid, and the three cuneiforms.

The calcaneum, os calcis, or heel-bone, is the largest of the tarsal bones. Its posterior portion, forming the prominence of the heel, receives the in-

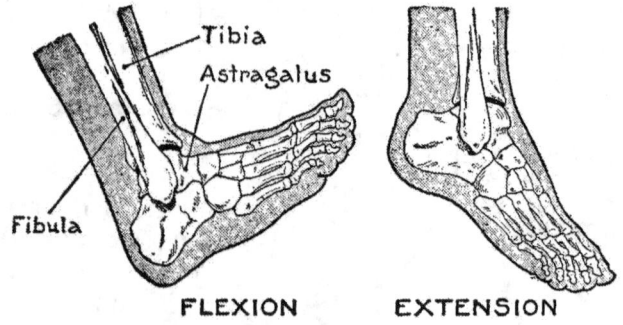

FLEXION   EXTENSION

THE HINGE-LIKE MOVEMENT THAT TAKES PLACE AT THE
ANKLE-JOINT.

sertion of the large tendon of Achilles. On its forward part it supports the astragalus, which can perhaps be considered as the principal ankle-bone, as it is the one that forms with the two leg-bones the articulation of the ankle.

The movement in the ankle-joint is like that of a hinge, in one plane only. This movement, consisting of extension and flexion, is the proper function of the joint, as the particular disposition of the bones hardly allows of anything else. The tibia and fibula ends, which are bound by ligaments, taken together resemble a clutch-like device grasping rather firmly the body of the astragalus.

The other tarsal bones—the scaphoid, immediately in front of the astragalus; the cuboid, on the little-toe side; and the three cuneiform enter into the structure of the arch of the foot. The completion of this structure is continued by the succeeding five metatarsal bones.

The phalanges which come next are the same in number and are arranged somewhat as the phalanges in the hand. The great toe, answering to the thumb, has, like it, two phalanges; while the rest of the toes, like the four fingers, have each three phalanges. And likewise, as in the hand, flexion and extension are the functional attributes of their respective joints.

But the resemblance in the skeletal plan of the hand and the foot is disturbed by the way the great-toe metatarsal is set and joins its tarsal bone. Instead of a saddle-joint, as in the thumb, it is by a simple articulation, permitting a form of flexion and extension only. Then it is not placed on the foot at that characteristic diverging angle exemplified in the position of the thumb on the hand.

The arched formation of the foot is one that especially pertains to man. This particular has, of course, to do with his erect position. The points of contact on the ground take on a character somewhat like that of a tripod: the heel, for instance, as one point of the tripod, the ball of the great toe, and the bones on the little toe side the other two. The

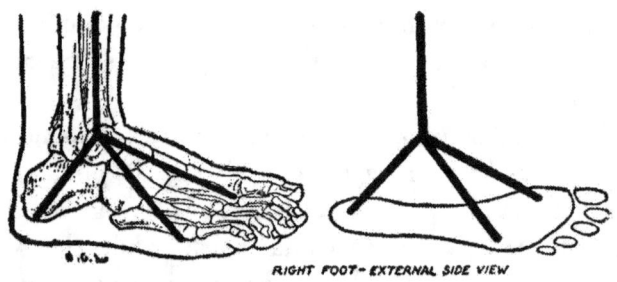

RIGHT FOOT- EXTERNAL SIDE VIEW

THE BONY STRUCTURE OF THE FOOT AS A TRIPOD.

top of the tripod is the ankle, where the weight of the body falls. All of the three arches between the tripodal points that rest on the ground are not distinguishable outwardly; only that from the heel to the ball of the great toe is clearly apparent.

As alluded to above, the bony structure plays the principal part in giving the "drawing" of the foot. This we see plainly in the dorsum of the foot. But as regards the sole, or plantar surface, we find the form filled out by paddings and cushions of fat, thick layers of integument, and groups of short muscles and tendons, no one particular having any special significance in creating the outer form. It is their combined mass laid on the skeleton founda-

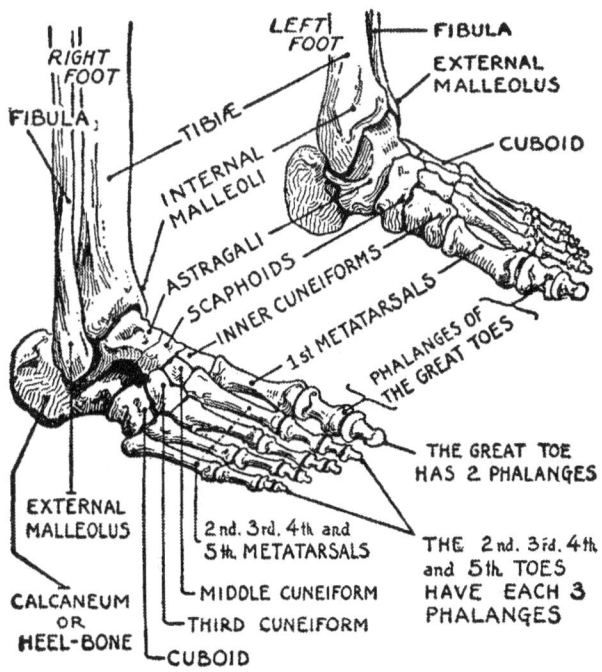

THE SKELETON OF THE FOOT IN DETAIL.

tion that gives the shape and roundness to the sole and borders of the foot.

In concluding our study of the osseous system of the body, we will mention in review the various parts of the skeletal division that we took up in this chapter, and which have some influence on the outer configuration.

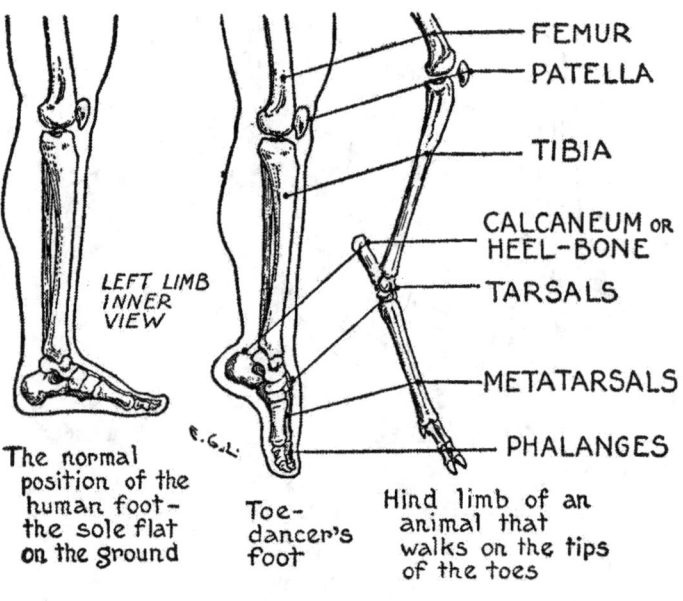

FEMUR
PATELLA
TIBIA
CALCANEUM OR HEEL-BONE
TARSALS
METATARSALS
PHALANGES

LEFT LIMB INNER VIEW

The normal position of the human foot— the sole flat on the ground

Toe-dancer's foot

Hind limb of an animal that walks on the tips of the toes

THE POINTS IN COMMON IN THE SKELETAL STRUCTURE OF THE LEG AND FOOT OF A BALLET-DANCER, AND IN THAT OF THE HIND LIMB OF AN ANIMAL THAT PROGRESSES ON THE TIPS OF THE TOES.

First, there is the great trochanter of the femur, and the hollow in the adjacent region back of it that is caused by the firmly stretched tendinous membrane of a muscle of the region.

In their order we will now further note:

In the region of the knee: The external and internal tuberosities of the femur.

The patella.

The external and internal tuberosities of the tibia.

The tubercle of the tibia.

The head of the fibula.

The leg : The subcutaneous surface of the tibia.

The ankle : The external malleolus and the internal malleolus.

The foot : The prominence of the heel.

The bony arch of the foot.

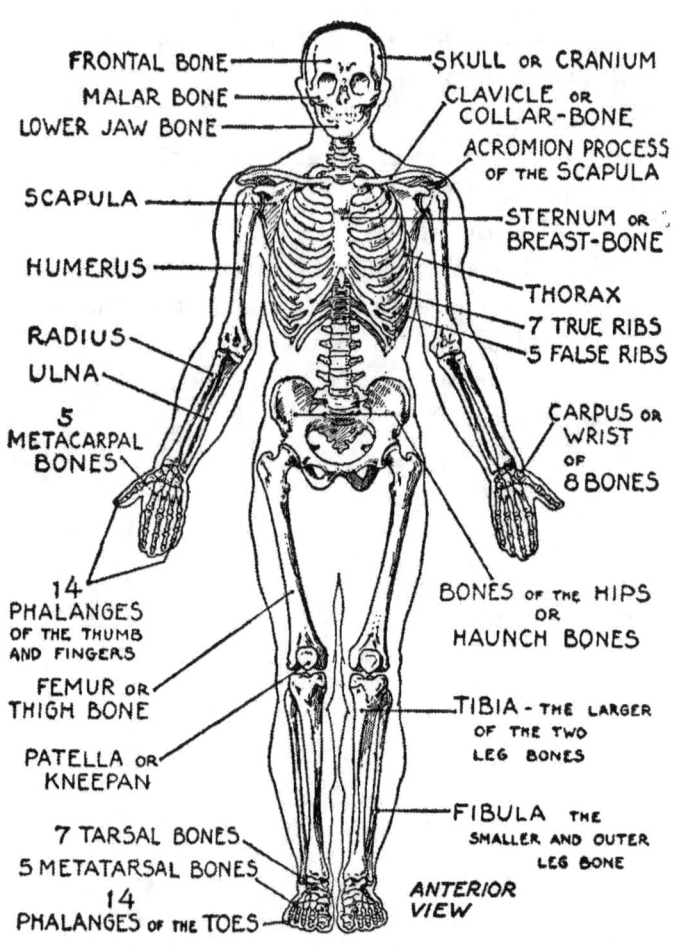

FRONTAL BONE

MALAR BONE

LOWER JAW BONE

SKULL or CRANIUM

CLAVICLE or COLLAR-BONE

ACROMION PROCESS of the SCAPULA

SCAPULA

HUMERUS

RADIUS

ULNA

5 METACARPAL BONES

STERNUM or BREAST-BONE

THORAX

7 TRUE RIBS

5 FALSE RIBS

CARPUS or WRIST OF 8 BONES

14 PHALANGES OF THE THUMB AND FINGERS

FEMUR or THIGH BONE

PATELLA or KNEEPAN

7 TARSAL BONES

5 METATARSAL BONES

14 PHALANGES of the TOES

BONES of the HIPS OR HAUNCH BONES

TIBIA - THE LARGER OF THE TWO LEG BONES

FIBULA THE SMALLER AND OUTER LEG BONE

ANTERIOR VIEW

THE SKELETON.

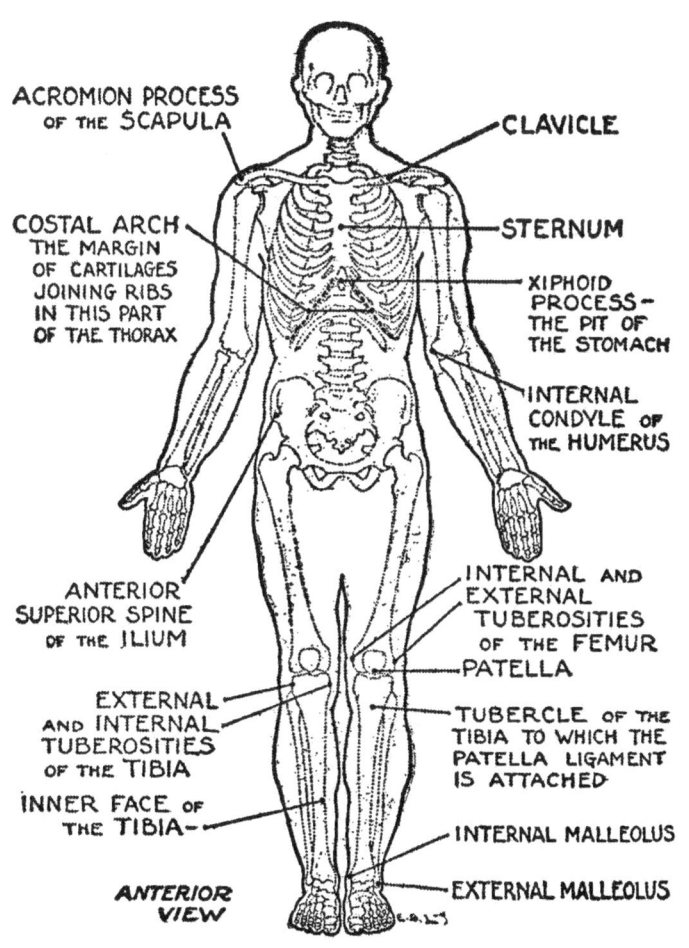

ACROMION PROCESS OF THE SCAPULA

CLAVICLE

COSTAL ARCH THE MARGIN OF CARTILAGES JOINING RIBS IN THIS PART OF THE THORAX

STERNUM

XIPHOID PROCESS — THE PIT OF THE STOMACH

INTERNAL CONDYLE OF THE HUMERUS

ANTERIOR SUPERIOR SPINE OF THE ILIUM

INTERNAL AND EXTERNAL TUBEROSITIES OF THE FEMUR

PATELLA

EXTERNAL AND INTERNAL TUBEROSITIES OF THE TIBIA

TUBERCLE OF THE TIBIA TO WHICH THE PATELLA LIGAMENT IS ATTACHED

INNER FACE OF THE TIBIA —

INTERNAL MALLEOLUS

EXTERNAL MALLEOLUS

ANTERIOR VIEW

WHERE THE BONES INFLUENCE THE OUTER FORM.

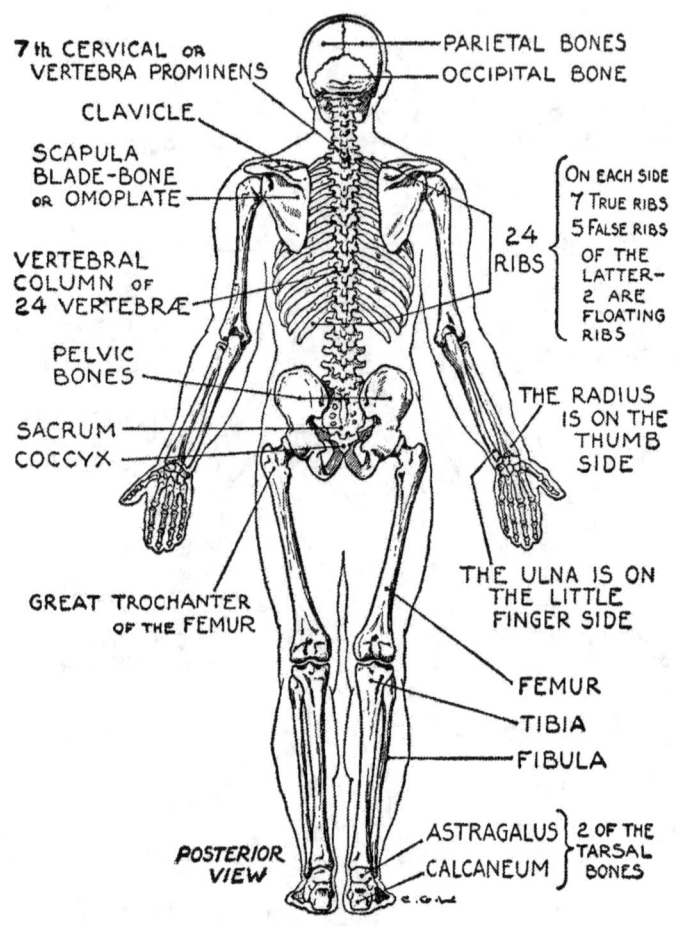

7th CERVICAL or
VERTEBRA PROMINENS

CLAVICLE

SCAPULA
BLADE-BONE
or OMOPLATE

VERTEBRAL
COLUMN of
24 VERTEBRÆ

PELVIC
BONES

SACRUM
COCCYX

GREAT TROCHANTER
OF THE FEMUR

PARIETAL BONES
OCCIPITAL BONE

ON EACH SIDE
7 TRUE RIBS
5 FALSE RIBS
OF THE
LATTER-
2 ARE
FLOATING
RIBS

24
RIBS

THE RADIUS
IS ON THE
THUMB
SIDE

THE ULNA IS ON
THE LITTLE
FINGER SIDE

FEMUR
TIBIA
FIBULA

ASTRAGALUS
CALCANEUM

2 OF THE
TARSAL
BONES

POSTERIOR
VIEW

THE SKELETON.

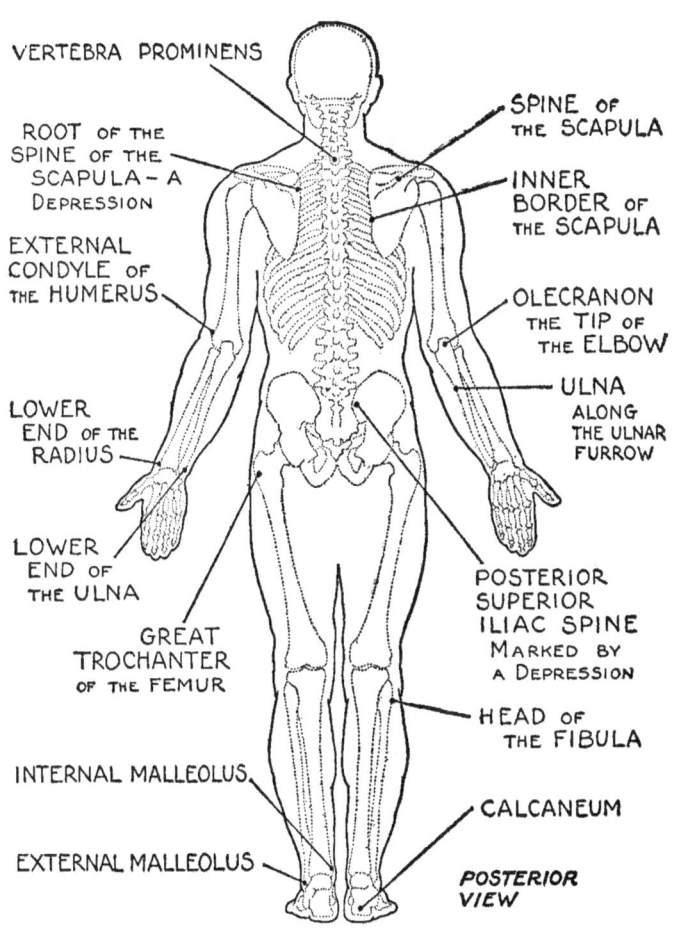

VERTEBRA PROMINENS

ROOT OF THE SPINE OF THE SCAPULA – A DEPRESSION

EXTERNAL CONDYLE OF THE HUMERUS

LOWER END OF THE RADIUS

LOWER END OF THE ULNA

GREAT TROCHANTER OF THE FEMUR

INTERNAL MALLEOLUS

EXTERNAL MALLEOLUS

SPINE OF THE SCAPULA

INNER BORDER OF THE SCAPULA

OLECRANON THE TIP OF THE ELBOW

ULNA ALONG THE ULNAR FURROW

POSTERIOR SUPERIOR ILIAC SPINE MARKED BY A DEPRESSION

HEAD OF THE FIBULA

CALCANEUM

POSTERIOR VIEW

WHERE THE BONES INFLUENCE THE OUTER FORM.

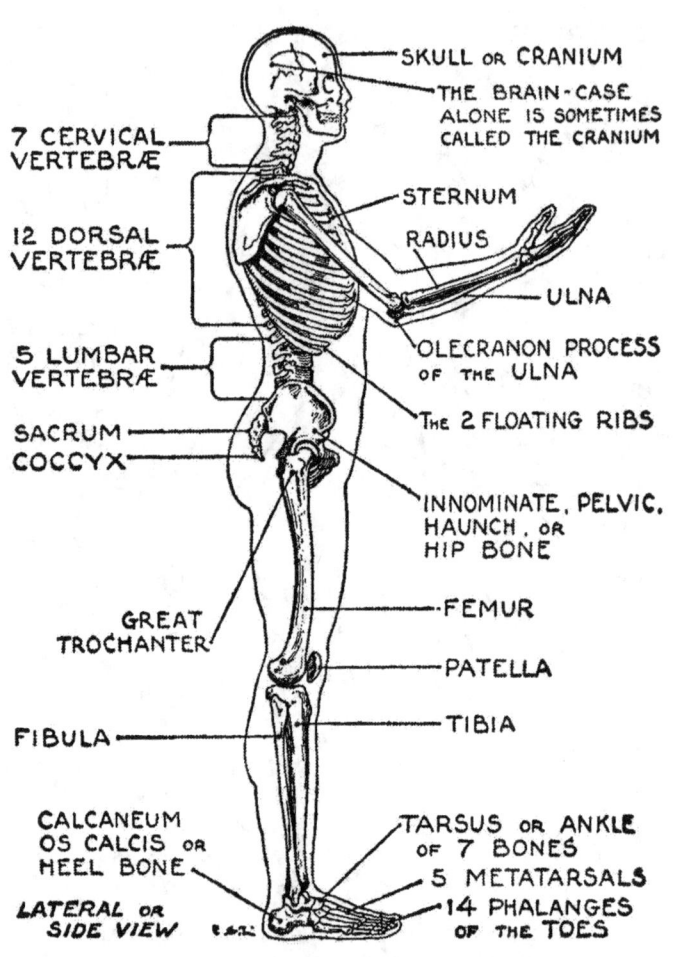

SKULL or CRANIUM

THE BRAIN-CASE
ALONE IS SOMETIMES
CALLED THE CRANIUM

7 CERVICAL
VERTEBRÆ

12 DORSAL
VERTEBRÆ

STERNUM

RADIUS

ULNA

OLECRANON PROCESS
OF THE ULNA

5 LUMBAR
VERTEBRÆ

THE 2 FLOATING RIBS

SACRUM
COCCYX

INNOMINATE, PELVIC,
HAUNCH, OR
HIP BONE

GREAT
TROCHANTER

FEMUR

PATELLA

TIBIA

FIBULA

CALCANEUM
OS CALCIS OR
HEEL BONE

TARSUS OR ANKLE
OF 7 BONES

5 METATARSALS

LATERAL OR
SIDE VIEW

14 PHALANGES
OF THE TOES

THE SKELETON.

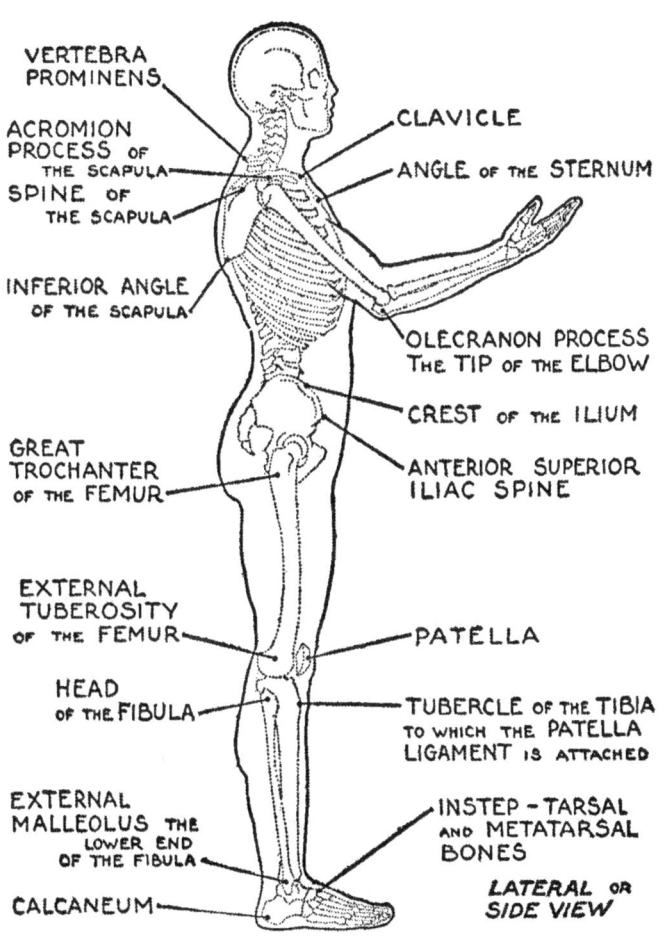

VERTEBRA PROMINENS

ACROMION PROCESS of THE SCAPULA

SPINE of THE SCAPULA

CLAVICLE

ANGLE of the STERNUM

INFERIOR ANGLE of THE SCAPULA

OLECRANON PROCESS THE TIP of THE ELBOW

CREST of the ILIUM

GREAT TROCHANTER of THE FEMUR

ANTERIOR SUPERIOR ILIAC SPINE

EXTERNAL TUBEROSITY of THE FEMUR

PATELLA

HEAD of THE FIBULA

TUBERCLE of THE TIBIA TO WHICH THE PATELLA LIGAMENT IS ATTACHED

EXTERNAL MALLEOLUS THE LOWER END OF THE FIBULA

INSTEP — TARSAL AND METATARSAL BONES

CALCANEUM

LATERAL OR *SIDE VIEW*

WHERE THE BONES INFLUENCE THE OUTER FORM.

PART TWO

THE GENERAL FORM OF THE BODY

VI

THE MUSCULAR SYSTEM

The Muscles in General

WE learned in the preceding part of the book the general facts relating to the structural framework of the body; that is to say an understanding of the character, positions, and arrangement of its separate parts, and an idea of the joints and their movements.

We will now proceed by taking up the elements that move this framework. Besides being the active organs of bodily power, these elements are the bulky parts that cover the bones and have the greater share in giving the figure roundnesses and contours. Both matters interest us, but the latter —that relating to relief and line—is the most important one for us. So the principal matter, then, with which we shall be concerned in the remaining chapters of the book is the general form of the body.

The muscular organs that put the bony frame into action are the skeletal muscles. This also includes the facial muscles that take part in, or give rise to, the expressions. These muscles in themselves take little part in giving form to the face;

but cause by their actions that infinite variety of expression peculiar to the human countenance.

The skeletal muscles that change the passive apparatus of bones into a moving structure of progression and movement owe their power to the con-

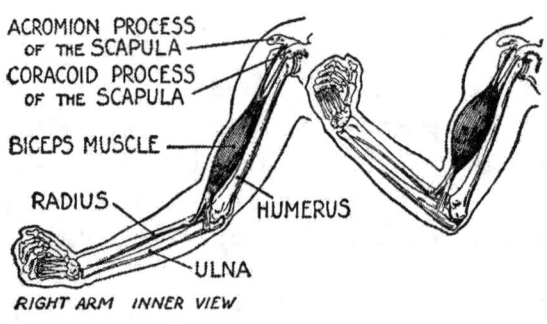

A MUSCLE IN ACTION.

tractile quality of their fibres. For us it is not necessary to go into the particulars of the construction of these fibres, or how the impulse to move any part of the living structure—say, a limb—passes along the various cords of the nervous system between the cerebral centres and the muscle. As artists, we are interested primarily in the typical form of a muscle, and how it changes this form during its various activities.

In simplest design most of the muscles that move the bones are elongated, with the middle section of fleshy fibres, called the belly, and with one or both

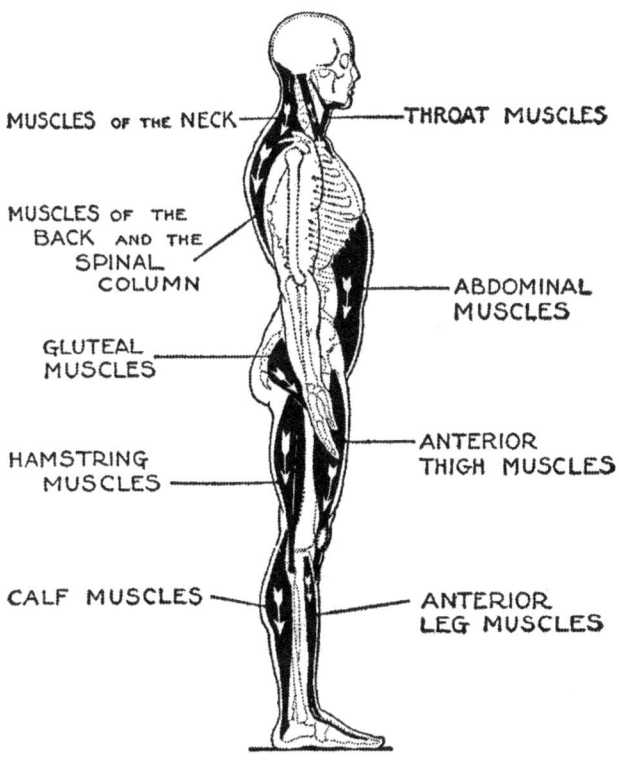

MUSCLES of the NECK

THROAT MUSCLES

MUSCLES of the BACK and the SPINAL COLUMN

ABDOMINAL MUSCLES

GLUTEAL MUSCLES

HAMSTRING MUSCLES

ANTERIOR THIGH MUSCLES

CALF MUSCLES

ANTERIOR LEG MUSCLES

EQUILIBRIUM IN STANDING IS MAINTAINED BY THE OPPOSING ACTIVITY OF THE MUSCLES OF THE ANTERIOR AND THE POSTERIOR REGIONS OF THE BODY.

Principal muscles concerned in this. The arrows indicate the direction of the force exerted.

ends tendinous. A typical example has one of these ends attached to a point called the origin, and the other to another point called the insertion. Between an origin and an insertion it is not possible at all times to make an exact distinction. The origin is held to be that point which is more or less stationary during the time that the muscle is in action, while the insertion is on a part that is moved by the active muscle. Generally, it is by a tendon

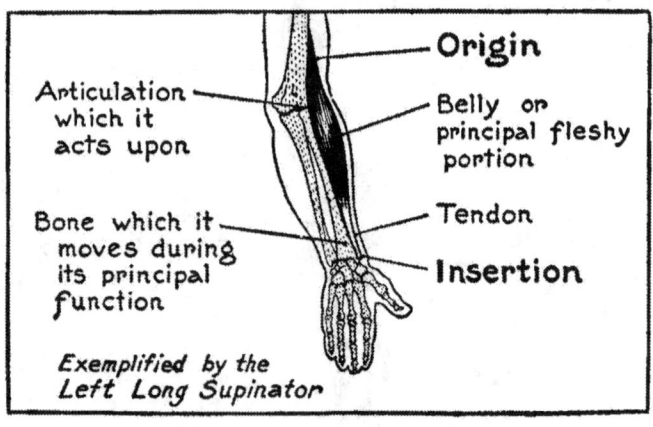

A TYPICAL STRUCTURAL MUSCLE.

that a muscle finds attachment to a bone, but oft-times the fleshy fibres are joined directly to the surface of a bone.

Muscles pass from one bone to a succeeding or an adjacent one. In the case of some of the limb muscles, they go to the second succeeding bone; that is, they skip one bone and pass over two artic-ulations.

Tendons are the cords or bands of dense tissue

terminating the muscular forms. When they are like cords and close to the skin they show as sinewy prominences. This is instanced on the front of the forearm, close to the wrist, and also, in thin persons, on the back of the hand. The tendon of the heel, or tendon of Achilles, at the back of the leg, is the largest and most conspicuous example in the human organism. Sometimes a tendon spreads out into a sheet of fibre called an aponeurosis. An aponeurotic layer gives to the region where it occurs a somewhat broad area.

Now, a muscle in itself is a bulging mass; roundness is its characteristic. And it should always be understood that this quality is typical of life. Convexity is the distinctive quality of the outer surface of the human figure; hollows should not be thought of as such, and emphasis always laid on the roundness of muscularity. Although some muscles are more or less in broad spreading layers, they cover with their fibrous expansions a convex or rounded region. The muscles of the back, abdomen, or the flank, for example.

The functional activity of a muscle is well illustrated by the perceptible mass on the anterior region of the upper arm. This, known to every one, is the biceps. Its fleshy fibres, when they contract, draw up the forearm toward the shoulder. The muscle has two origins beneath the shoulder muscle mass; while below, one tendon goes to the radius and another one expands into an aponeurosis that is merged with other membranes on the forearm.

Muscles are nearly all arranged to have others as antagonists. Or there are antagonistic groups of

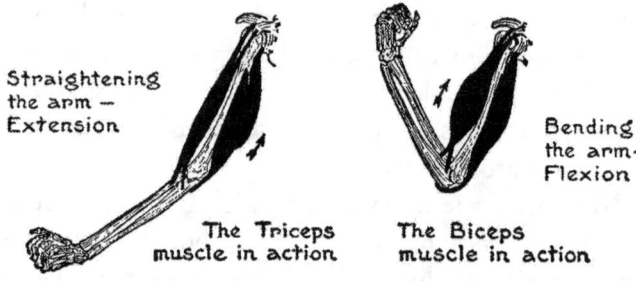

Straightening
the arm —
Extension

Bending
the arm—
Flexion

The Triceps
muscle in action

The Biceps
muscle in action

A PAIR OF ANTAGONISTIC MUSCLES IN ACTION.

muscles. Now in the case of the biceps, when its fleshy portion swells out to move the forearm, a muscle on the back of the limb, the triceps, relaxes its fibres. But when the triceps, in straightening the arm, proceeds to pull on the forearm, the biceps in its turn must relax. Of course, in this instance other muscles take part in the movement; but this particular case is one of the less complex and a fitting example to illustrate the principle of antagonistic muscles.

THE DIFFERENT REGIONS OF THE BODY

Before we go on with the study of the muscular system we will direct our thoughts to a few matters that will help us in our work. First is this: to have always, while we are trying to acquire a knowledge of the human figure, a clear understanding of the defining and descriptive terms used, and when certain regions are named in treating of a muscle, to know exactly to what region the particular name refers.

Besides, in the matter of nomenclature, muscular forms are named according to their function or shape; or, again, with regard to the region that they occupy. All these are matters that, if we remember them, will help to keep a visual picture in the mind of the shape and location, and an idea of the function of any muscle in question.

Muscles are spoken of as belonging to a particular surface—anterior, posterior, lateral or external, and medial or internal. By internal, or medial, is meant that region or surface close to, or toward the median line—that imaginary line dividing the whole figure into two symmetrical halves.

The ordinary divisions of the human figure into that of trunk, limbs, head, and neck are clearly understood and intelligible. But, on the other hand, when we come to the various subdivisions—

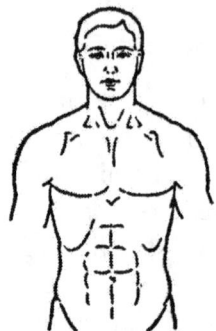

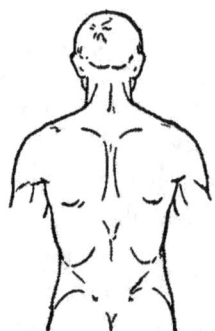

Front anterior { View surface
or ventral.   { or region.

Back posterior { View surface
or dorsal.   { or region.

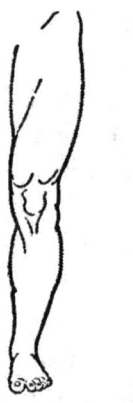

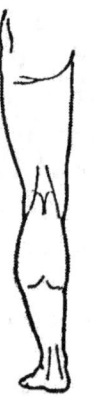

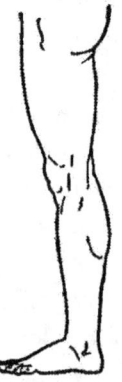

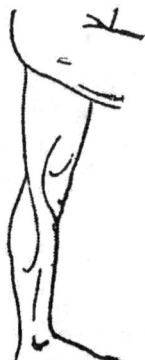

Front or   { View or
anterior. { surface.

Back or   { View or
posterior. { surface.

Outer
external   { View or
or lateral. { surface.

Inner
internal   { View or
or medial. { surface.

TERMS DESIGNATING THE RELATIVE POSITION OF PARTS OF
THE BODY.

parts of the trunk, for instance, we are not at all times so sure as to the precise signification of the terms. A little summary on this subject would perhaps not be out of place.

Torso is sometimes used to denote the human trunk, but ordinarily in the arts this word is employed to describe a sculptural piece—especially one from classical times representing the human trunk, generally fragmentary with parts of the limbs remaining. We had best in our study adhere to the simple term trunk, and leave the word torso to its use as applied in the plastic art. Thorax includes in its descriptive signification the whole upper part of the trunk. To be precise, though, it should be restricted to that part that has as its foundation the bony cage composed of the twelve pairs of ribs, the sternum, and the dorsal region of the back-bone.

The term chest can also be applied to the thorax; but commonly, when we use this word, we have reference to the front part of the thorax.

The breast is easy to define, it is plainly that part of the thorax covered by the two large pectoral muscles; its lower limit is well marked in muscular subjects by the relief of the lower borders of these muscles. These borders are at about the level of the fifth or sixth rib.

The armpit, or axilla, changes its form. We picture it as a hollow beneath the shoulder when the

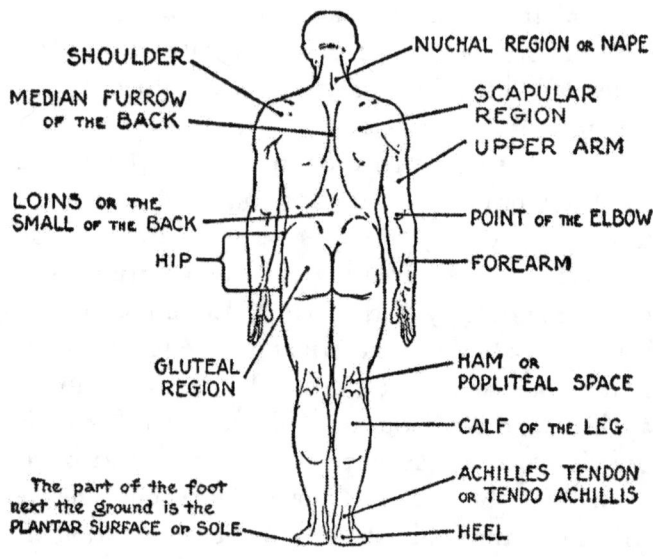

REGIONS AND PARTS OF THE HUMAN BODY.

arm is raised, with folds of muscle forming two walls in front and back.

The divisions of the upper limb, or superior extremity, are those of upper arm, forearm, wrist, and hand.

The sharp angle of the olecranon process of the ulna represents the tip, or point, of the elbow. In front at the bend of the elbow is a depression which may be styled either the pit or the hollow of the elbow. In flexion, the hollow of the elbow disappears when the muscles of the region come together.

The appellation of the palm of the hand is perfectly clear, to be sure, and likewise the back of the hand. The term dorsum, or dorsal surface, can also be applied in the latter case.

The more or less triangular area of the back of the neck corresponding to the superior portion of the trapezius, the large muscle of the back, is the nuchal region, or the nape.

The borders of the scapular region would coincide with the underlying outlines of the scapula.

The region of the shoulder encroaches partly on the neck, the breast, the scapular region, and on the arm. But it can be best thought of as limited by the contours of the mass of the large shoulder muscle—the deltoid.

On the middle of the back is a trough-like formation that passes downward to be lost in the lower lumbar region. This formation, due to the bulging of the strong muscular masses placed on each side of the row of vertebral spines, is called the median furrow of the back.

There are hardly any well-defining lines or characteristics to indicate the flank clearly. This area can be considered as the side of the trunk immediately above the iliac crest of the hip-bone.

The hip would include as much of the lower side of the trunk that has as its skeletal structure the wing-like iliac portion of the hip-bone.

The abdominal region is limited above by the thoracic, or costal, arch, which marks the line of the costal cartilages of the two sides of the thorax. Often in classical sculpture this is given a very round form, rather than a modified curve proper to the human figure. The lower borders of the abdomen are marked by the groins, those oblique furrows that go from without, inward and downward to the middle of the figure. The line of a groin represents outwardly the place and direction of a membrane called Poupart's ligament, an anatomical feature that we have already commented upon in our study of the pelvis.

The gluteal region is formed by that quadrilateral mass of muscle at the lower region of the back of the trunk. At its lower border is the gluteal fold, which separates it from the posterior region of the thigh. Laterally it extends to the area adjacent to the great trochanter of the femur.

The thigh, the first segment of the lower limb, very plainly marked off from the trunk on the anterior region by the groin, and posteriorly by the fold of the gluteal mass, is not, however, definitely distinguished from the hips on the lateral region.

The region of the knee includes the patella and the adjacent regions that take part in the articulation. The space immediately back of the knee is given the more specific term of ham. It is also

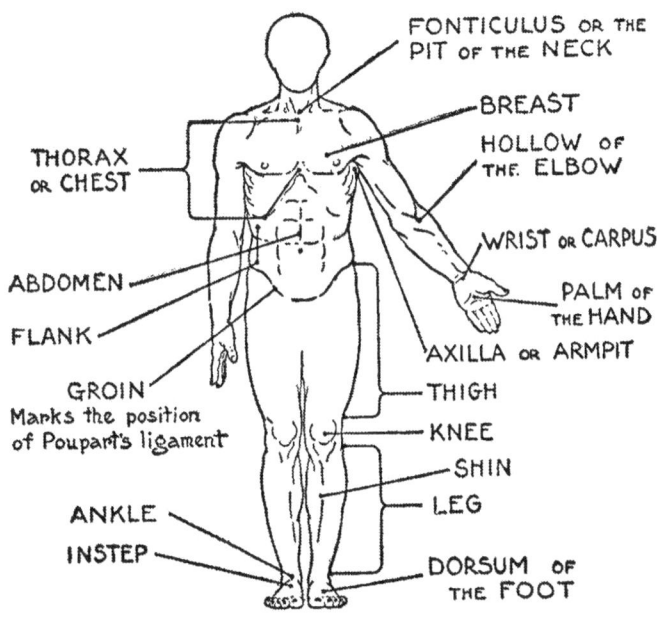

FONTICULUS OR THE PIT OF THE NECK

BREAST

HOLLOW OF THE ELBOW

THORAX OR CHEST

WRIST OR CARPUS

PALM OF THE HAND

ABDOMEN

FLANK

AXILLA OR ARMPIT

GROIN
Marks the position of Poupart's ligament

THIGH

KNEE

SHIN

LEG

ANKLE

INSTEP

DORSUM OF THE FOOT

REGIONS AND PARTS OF THE HUMAN BODY.

called the popliteal space. Ham also denotes the fleshy part of the back of the thigh.

The division of the lower limb between the knee and the foot is, according to its strict anatomical definition, the leg. (Commonly, and in every-day speech, we use this term to mean the whole limb.) The calf is the muscular prominence on the back of the leg. It is occasioned by the two muscles of the posterior region of the leg that send down that thick tendinous cord—the tendon of Achilles.

We have already commented on the two malleoli, that form the prominences of the ankle. It should be remembered that the ankle, or tarsal, bones are directly below this region that we usually think of as the ankle.

The back, top, or dorsum of the foot has as its structural basis the anterior tarsal and the metatarsal bones. It is on the sole of the foot, or plantar surface, that the human subject walks. Hence it is that he is placed, along with the bear, among the plantigrade animals, in opposition, according to the naturalists, to the digitigrade creatures that move along on the tips of their foot bones.

As to the Movements of the Body

Another matter that will help us in our study, and which we will go over briefly, is the nature of the different movements of the body and its members.

When a muscle is put into action there results movement with something practical effected—moving a limb, perhaps—or one of the phases of some form of progression. This movement is called the function of the muscle, and as we must attend to a matter of this kind in our study, as well as the muscular form and its peculiarities, we will devote a little time to a consideration of the terms used in describing the various movements.

It is clear, to be sure, that bending the arm at the elbow is flexion, and that unbending it to straighten it out is extension. When the straightened-out arm is dropped to the side of the body it is called adduction, and when from this position it

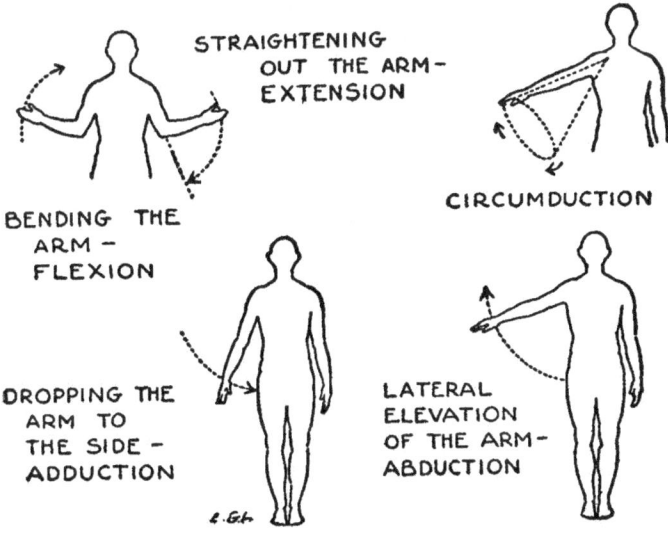

STRAIGHTENING
OUT THE ARM–
EXTENSION

BENDING THE
ARM –
FLEXION

CIRCUMDUCTION

DROPPING THE
ARM TO
THE SIDE –
ADDUCTION

LATERAL
ELEVATION
OF THE ARM–
ABDUCTION

MOVEMENTS OF THE UPPER LIMB.

is moved away from the side of the body it is abduction. It will be a simple matter to remember the distinction between these two terms. The prefix *ad* means to; while *ab* means away from. The root of the word is of Latin origin—*ducere*, to lead. In these movements of adduction and abduction the arm is moved toward or away from the median line of the body. These movements also take place and are similarly named in the lower limb.

If the arm is held straight out and moved so that the tips of the fingers describe a circle in the air, it is circumduction. The arm and hand in this action describe an imaginary cone; the apex of the cone corresponding to the shoulder-joint and the base bounded by the circle in the air. The lower limb, too, is capable of circumduction; the joint at the hip answering to the apex, while the toes describe the imaginary base of the cone.

The action when the foot is raised from the ground and the whole leg is straight and turned on its own axis is called rotation. This, however, is not as free a movement as the word rotation implies in its fullest sense. Rotation can also be carried out in the arm.

The turning of the head from side to side as it rests on the top of and moves with the atlas vertebra, while this latter bone pivots on the odontoid process of the axis, is another example of rotation.

When the thigh is moved toward the front of the trunk it is flexion; and when the whole limb is moved in the same direction it is also flexion.

Bending the knee and moving the leg toward the back of the thigh is flexion; while, on the other hand, if the entire limb is moved backward as if trying

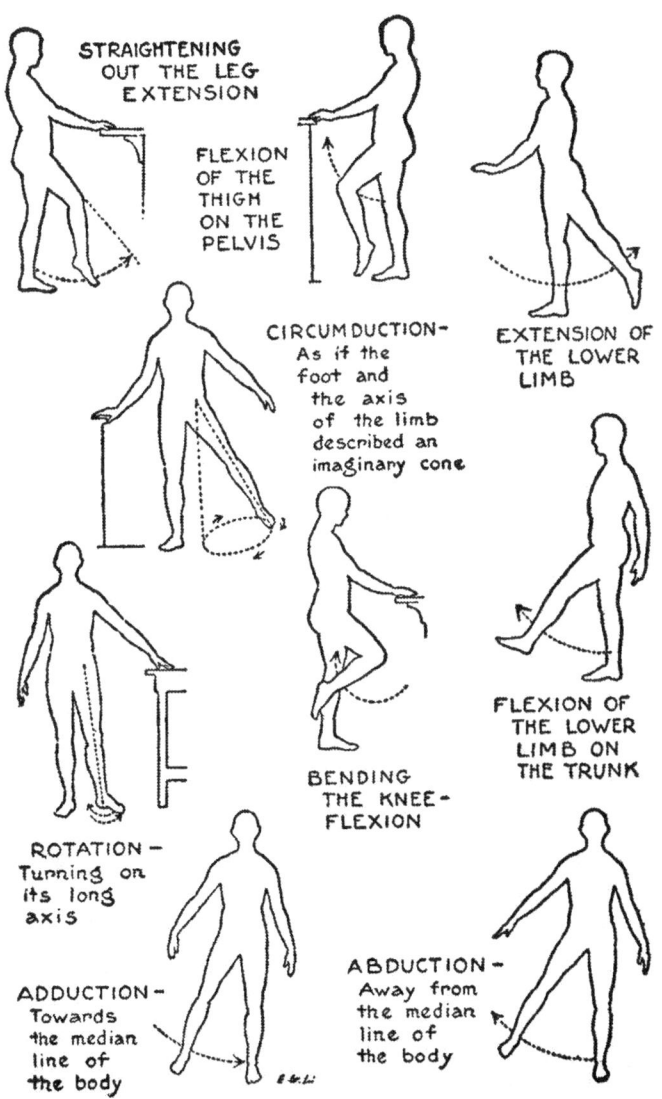

STRAIGHTENING OUT THE LEG EXTENSION

FLEXION OF THE THIGH ON THE PELVIS

CIRCUMDUCTION—As if the foot and the axis of the limb described an imaginary cone

EXTENSION OF THE LOWER LIMB

FLEXION OF THE LOWER LIMB ON THE TRUNK

BENDING THE KNEE—FLEXION

ROTATION—Turning on its long axis

ADDUCTION—Towards the median line of the body

ABDUCTION—Away from the median line of the body

MOVEMENTS OF THE LOWER LIMB.

to kick with our heels, it is extension. Straightening out the flexed, or bent, knee is extension.

When in the standing position we bend the body forward at the hips, in a hinge-like bow, we have flexion of the trunk on the lower limbs. If the

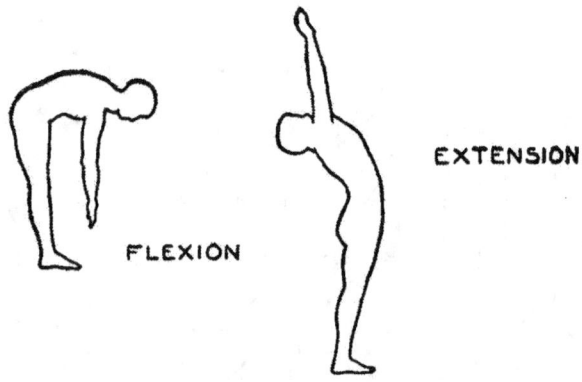

FLEXION

EXTENSION

MOVEMENTS OF THE TRUNK.

bending is at the waist between the hips and the thorax it is flexion of the trunk. Any movement backward to the straight position in both cases is, of course, extension. When we lean back as far as we can, as if stretching ourselves, it is extension.

Bending the hand at the wrist and moving it in the direction of the front of the forearm is flexion. In going back—the contrary direction—it is extension. Now moving the hand at the wrist in the direction of the radial side we have another example

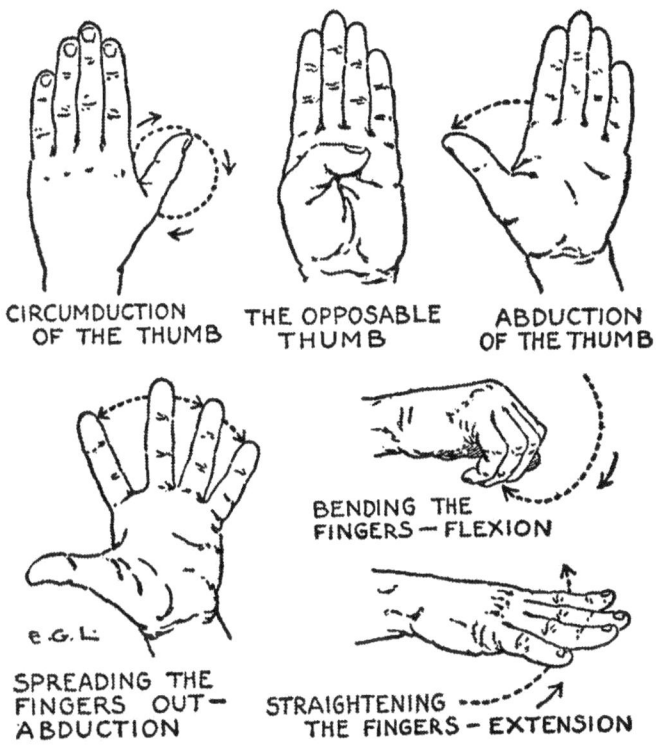

CIRCUMDUCTION
OF THE THUMB

THE OPPOSABLE
THUMB

ABDUCTION
OF THE THUMB

BENDING THE
FINGERS — FLEXION

SPREADING THE
FINGERS OUT—
ABDUCTION

STRAIGHTENING
THE FINGERS — EXTENSION

e.G.L.

MOVEMENTS OF THE DIGITS.

of abduction, while toward the ulnar side it is adduction.

Seemingly inconsistent is the nomenclature used
in describing the movements of the toes and the
foot. When the foot is straightened out, and the
angle that the dorsum makes with the front of the

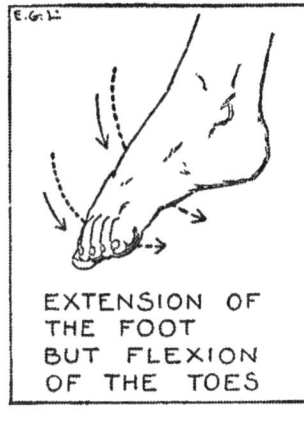 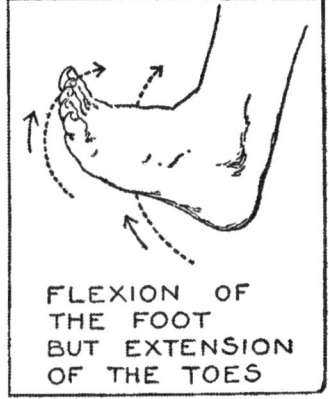

EXTENSION OF THE FOOT BUT FLEXION OF THE TOES

FLEXION OF THE FOOT BUT EXTENSION OF THE TOES

CONCURRENT MOVEMENT IN THE SAME DIRECTION IN THE FOOT AND TOES HAS TWO DESCRIPTIVE TERMS.

which the angle at the ankle is decreased, it is flexion of the foot, and when the toes follow in the same direction—upward toward the leg—they are in extension.

The Order of Our Study of the Muscular System

In our study of the muscles we will proceed in a similar way, generally, as that followed in the chapters on the osseous parts of the body. We began there with the spinal column, and so now in the next chapter the first muscular form to be considered will be that which plays the principal part in holding this spinal column in place and at its proper and normal curvature.

Our inquiry continues by the study of the other muscles of the back, being next in importance, as they act on the spinal column, too.   Then when the rest of the muscular forms that cover the skeleton of the trunk—thorax and pelvis—have been taken up, we will proceed to the head and neck, the skeletal foundation of which regions, as we know, belong to the axial division of the bony framework. Then we will consider, to complete our subject, the muscular systems of the upper and the lower limbs.

VII

THE MUSCLES OF THE TRUNK

The Back

THE DEEP MUSCLES OF THE SPINE

(Erector spinæ)*

(Sacrospinalis)†

WE have learned in our study of the skeleton that there are two grooves on the posterior region of the bony thorax separated from each other by the middle line of the back, which line follows the row of vertebral spines. The outer limits of these grooves correspond to the lines of the angles of the ribs from the second to the eleventh pairs. These grooves are filled up in the living by bundles of muscular and tendinous fibres that constitute the superior portions of large fleshy masses and aponeu-

---

* Whenever it seemed that the anatomical text-book name of a muscle was one readily comprehended it is used in this work. In other instances more easily grasped terms are employed. In these latter cases the anatomical names are given in parentheses at the heads of their proper paragraphs.

† Scientific terminology varies. In certain cases when a muscular form has still another name, it is put in a second parenthesis. Anatomical terms are noted, as a means of identification, in case any one wishes to go into the subject more thoroughly than it is presented in this book. The word "musculus" is presupposed to go before each scientific name of a muscle.

123

rotic tissue called the *erectores spinæ*. There are three main divisions of an erector spinæ of one side: the ILIOCOSTAL portion, lying externally; the LONGISSIMUS DORSI, coming next; and the SPINALIS DORSI portion, close to the row of vertebral spines.

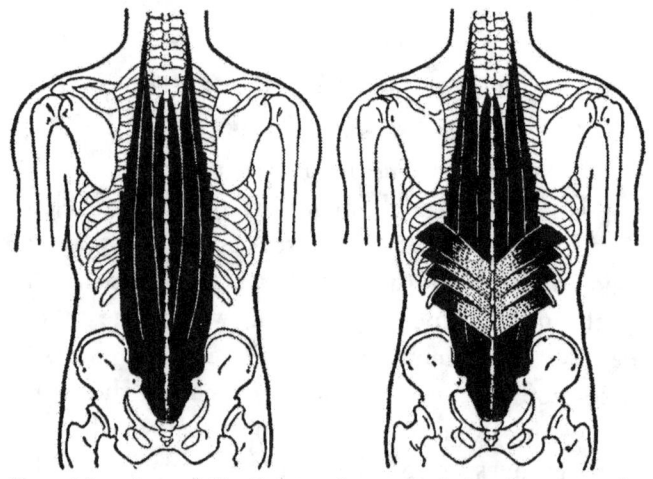

Deep Muscles of the Spine   Lower Posterior Serrati Muscles

TWO DEEP-LAYER MUSCULAR FORMS OF THE BACK.

It is not necessary that the artist memorize the names of the divisions of this muscular form; he only needs to keep in mind that they form one columnar mass of deep muscles of the spine, and that they cause, with the mass of the other side, those bulgings out to form between them the median furrow of the back. These muscles arise from the posterior portions of the iliac bones and the sacrum, in which region they form one common tendinous part which extends to the limit of the loins, where the fleshy fibres begin to divide near the lower thorax into fleshy slips and tendons that pass upward to attachments on the vertebral processes, up to and including the lower cervical vertebræ. Slips of fibres find attachment to the ribs also.

The deep muscles of the spine, besides extending the trunk, or bringing it back to its proper position after it has been flexed, help to keep the whole body in the erect position.   They are also effective elements in retaining the back-bone in its normal degree of curvature.

This muscular division is covered in its upper part by other muscles, and below by the aponeurotic portions of the two latissimus dorsi muscles. This latter muscle is the important anatomical detail of the lower region of the back.   But before we proceed with its study we will note a small deep muscle, the LOWER POSTERIOR SERRATUS (*serratus posticus inferior*).   At the lower region of the thorax, where it is found, it finds attachment to some lower ribs by slips coming from the last dorsal and a few lumbar vertebræ.   This lower serratus does not often modify the outer form, but it is required that we mention it.   Sometimes its relief is observable on very muscular subjects, or it can be perceived, when its fibres are stretched, in flexion of the trunk, through the layers of the superimposed latissimus dorsi.

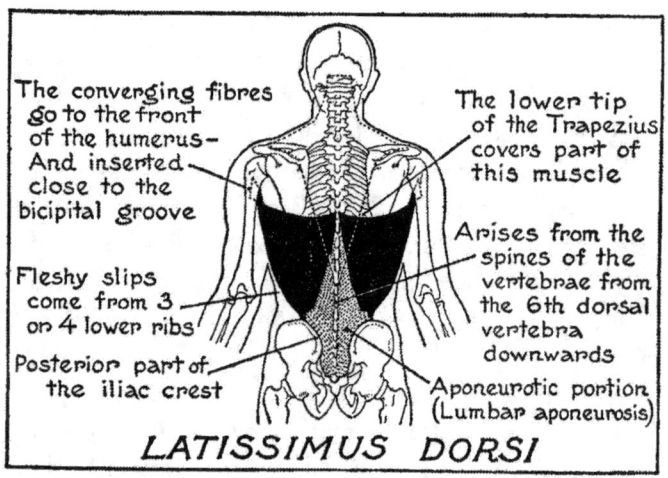

The converging fibres go to the front of the humerus — And inserted close to the bicipital groove

The lower tip of the Trapezius covers part of this muscle

Arises from the spines of the vertebrae from the 6th dorsal vertebra downwards

Fleshy slips come from 3 or 4 lower ribs

Posterior part of the iliac crest

Aponeurotic portion (Lumbar aponeurosis)

LATISSIMUS DORSI

LATISSIMUS DORSI

This, the broad muscle covering the lower part of the back, reaches from the sacrum to the middle of the trunk, and laterally to the armpit. It is a superficial layer of fibre. The lower portion in the sacral region is aponeurotic, and forms, with the corresponding portion on the other side, the lumbar aponeurosis. The region that this aponeurotic portion covers is the small of the back, or the loins.

The muscle finds attachments to the sacrum, the

posterior crest of the ilium, the lumbar, and the last six dorsal vertebræ. It is inserted into the humerus, along the inner ridge bordering the bicipital groove. Where the fleshy fibres begin, that is, where they arise from the aponeurosis at the small of the back, there is marked on the outer form a bulging line or relief. This relief extends from the ilium obliquely, upward and inward, toward the dorsal vertebræ. Toward the lateral side where the muscle approaches the place of its insertion into the arm-bone, it narrows and its fibres twist upon themselves. The lateral border as it runs upward obliquely across the flank forms a marked feature on the outer surface, especially so when the arm is raised, or the model is hanging from a trapeze. The superior border that runs nearly horizontally across the back at the level of the sixth or seventh dorsal vertebra passes over the inferior angle of the scapula. Thus the latissimus dorsi helps to hold the scapula close to the thorax. Sometimes, too, as the muscle passes over the scapula, a few fibres affix themselves to the bone. Other slips of fibres are joined to the lower three or four ribs.

In action, the latissimus dorsi pulls the shoulder down. It draws the raised arm down to the side of the body. It comes into play, and is brought out in prominence, in such exercises as climbing a rope or raising oneself on a horizontal bar.

The upper middle part of the muscle, that small section joining the last six dorsal vertebræ, is covered by the downward-pointing tip of the large muscle of the superior region of the back, and which comes next in the order of our study.

TRAPEZIUS

With the exception of part of the shoulder and a triangular area in the scapular region, the whole superficial fleshy formation of the back is composed of the latissimus dorsi and this muscle that now comes under our notice. This, the trapezius, is found on the back of the neck, shoulder, and part of the posterior thoracic region. Its inner border along the middle line extends from the head to the last, or twelfth, dorsal vertebra. Outwardly it extends to the summit of the shoulder, where it passes around anteriorly to the clavicle. Its insertion into the clavicle is along its outer third of the shaft. The two muscles of both sides taken together give an outline resembling a monk's cowl that has been thrown back over the shoulders. Hence a name by which this muscle is sometimes distinguished: CUCULLARIS (Latin, *cucullus*, a hood).

The trapezius shows on the outer aspect several depressions that are caused by certain aponeurotic areas, their visibility conditioned, of course, by the muscular development of the particular subject.

There is one tiny area at the very tip of the monk's cowl, or that lower point which covers the upper part of the latissimus dorsi. Another is found at the base of the spine of the scapula, which aponeurotic area glides over the bone there when the muscle

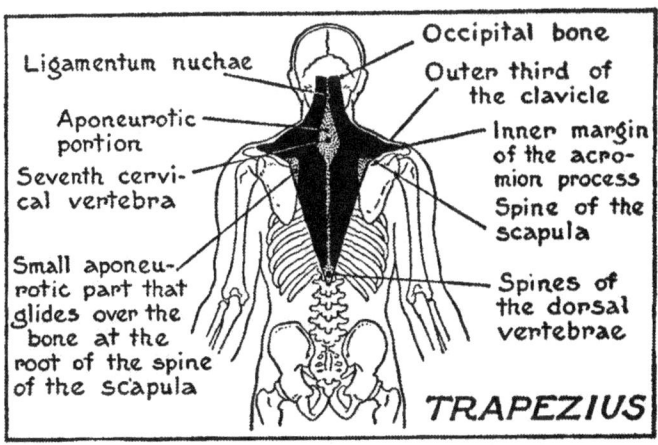

Ligamentum nuchae

Aponeurotic portion

Seventh cervical vertebra

Small aponeurotic part that glides over the bone at the root of the spine of the scapula

Occipital bone

Outer third of the clavicle

Inner margin of the acromion process

Spine of the scapula

Spines of the dorsal vertebrae

TRAPEZIUS

is in action. An important area is that surrounding the vertebra prominens at the base of the neck; it is elliptical in shape, and is formed by the combined aponeuroses of the two trapezii. The ligamentum nuchæ, a firm fibrous part that stretches from the occiput to some of the vertebral spines and helps to hold the head in place, separates the nuchal portions of the trapezii. The ligament also affords attachment to fibres of the muscle. In some cases there is, on the middle line directly over the ligamentum nuchæ, a depression marking the division between the two muscles. Here, in moving the head up and down, the tense tissue of the ligament can be felt by the fingers.

The upper part of the trapezius on the lateral region gives the contours of the neck as viewed from various aspects. There are, though, no hard outlines; they have been softened by the way in which the muscle rounds gently over the shoulder to the clavicular insertion.

On account of the extent and the varying directions of its fibres the muscle's function depends upon the particular part that is in action. The nuchal part, if the shoulders are fixed, will pull the head back, but if only one side of this part is in function the head will be drawn to the side of this part.

The entire muscle, to be sure, with its free portions joined to the easily moved shoulder girdle—scapulæ and clavicles—acts very strongly on the shoulders. The upper portions will pull the shoulders up—shrugging them—while the lower portions will draw them down, and the middle fibres, acting antagonistically, will cause the scapulæ to approach each other.

As we have remarked, the forms of the latissimus dorsi and trapezius muscles, with the exceptions of

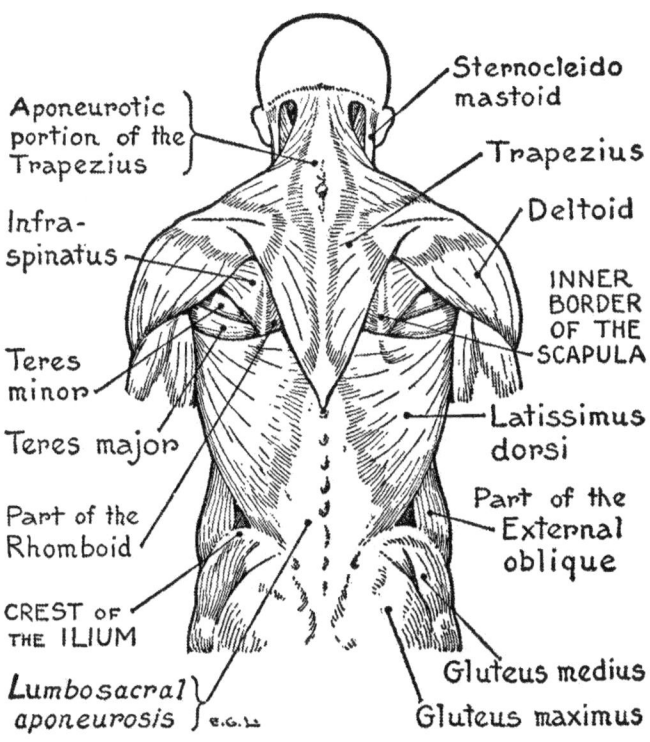

Sternocleido mastoid

Aponeurotic portion of the Trapezius

Trapezius

Infra-spinatus

Deltoid

INNER BORDER OF THE SCAPULA

Teres minor

Teres major

Latissimus dorsi

Part of the Rhomboid

Part of the External oblique

CREST OF THE ILIUM

Lumbosacral aponeurosis

Gluteus medius

Gluteus maximus

THE MUSCLES OF THE BACK OF THE TRUNK.

certain parts of the shoulders and triangular areas in the scapular regions, cover the whole of the back.

Now in these triangular areas four scapular muscles show parts of their forms directly beneath the skin. Their distinguishing traits, as far as they concern artists, will be studied in the following few paragraphs.

The Scapular Region
rhomboid
(Comprising the *Rhomboideus minor* and the *Rhomboideus major*)

When the arm is hanging by the side, one of the areas alluded to above is outlined below by the nearly horizontal upper border of the latissimus

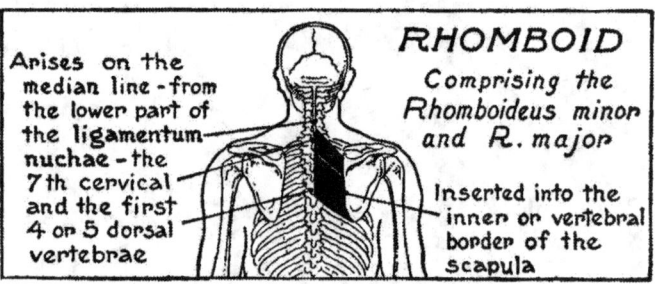

Arises on the median line - from the lower part of the ligamentum nuchae - the 7th cervical and the first 4 or 5 dorsal vertebrae

RHOMBOID
Comprising the Rhomboideus minor and R. major

Inserted into the inner or vertebral border of the scapula

dorsi; on the inner side by the trapezius, and outwardly by the posterior edge of the deltoid, or shoulder muscle.

Now the rhomboid shows but a very small part of its fibres within this area. Those that do appear are found at its lower inner angle. The rhomboid arises from the back-bone, from the last neck to the fourth or the fifth dorsal vertebra, and passes obliquely downward to the inner, or vertebral, border of the scapula. In action it pulls this bone upward and toward the middle line. Although nearly

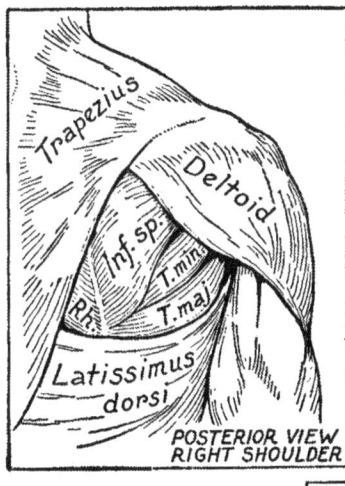

Inf. sp.
Infraspinatus

T. min.
Teres minor

T. maj.
Teres major

Rh. Rhomboid

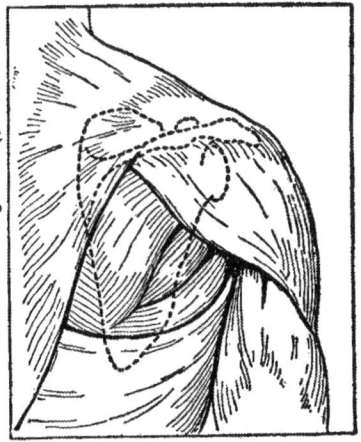

The scapula
with reference
to the
overlying muscles

The dotted lines
show its
position

DIAGRAM TO SHOW THE POSITION OF THE SCAPULA AND THE
RELATION OF THE MUSCULATURE THAT COVERS IT.

completely covered by the trapezius, its bulging
form influences the outer relief and helps by its
mass, with that of the other side, to emphasize the
median furrow of the back.

INFRASPINATUS

The inferior part of the posterior surface of the
scapula is named its lower fossa. The greater part
of this fossa is occupied by the infraspinatus, or the
muscle below the spine. This muscle, from its
origin within this fossa, goes outwardly to be inserted into the large tuberosity of the humerus.
Its function is to rotate the bone outwardly and
pull the arm back. The subcutaneous portion is
bordered by the teres minor.

TERES MINOR

This is a small round muscle of the lower fossa
of the scapula, it co-ordinates with the infraspinatus,
and, like it, is fixed to the posterior surface of the
humerus. The two insertions adjoin one another.

TERES MAJOR

This is the larger round muscle of the lower
scapular fossa. It borders the teres minor muscle,
and shows, subcutaneously, more of its fibres than
the smaller form.

From its origin on the inferior angle of the scapula it passes to the front of the humerus, to be inserted into the anterior surface. This is in direct contrast to the insertions of the last two muscles, which, as we have noted, found attachment to the posterior

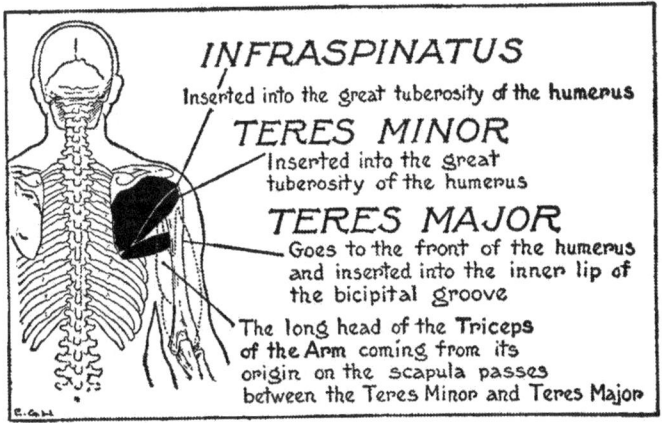

INFRASPINATUS
Inserted into the great tuberosity of the humerus

TERES MINOR
Inserted into the great tuberosity of the humerus

TERES MAJOR
Goes to the front of the humerus and inserted into the inner lip of the bicipital groove

The long head of the Triceps of the Arm coming from its origin on the scapula passes between the Teres Minor and Teres Major

The three muscles of the lower fossa of the scapula

surface. As we can see from the nature of its insertion, the teres major rotates the arm inwardly as well as pulling it back.

These three scapular muscles of which we have given the preceding account are put on the stretch and lengthened when the arm is thrust forward or upward. And, when the arm is forced backward and rotated, their contracting fibres make reliefs in this region. The teres major, especially in its

contracted state, or strongly developed, shows as
a well-rounded form that softens the angle of division where the muscle of the back of the arm springs
out of the shoulder mass. In movements of the
arm in which the axilla shows its form and depth,

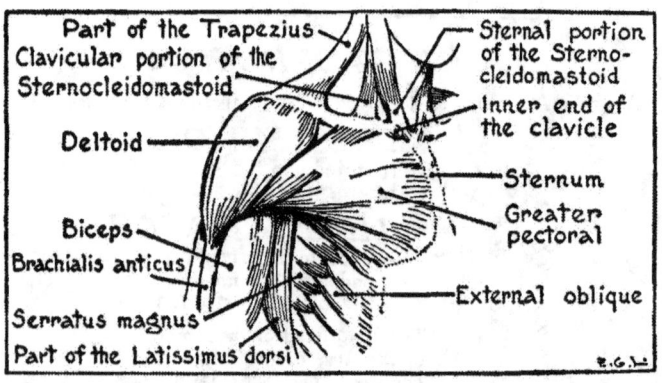

THE MUSCLES OF THE RIGHT SHOULDER AND ADJACENT REGIONS.

the action of the teres major should be observed
as it follows the axillary portion of the latissimus
dorsi. The insertions of these two muscles are in
contact where they join the arm-bone.

THE SHOULDER AND THE CHEST

DELTOID
(*Deltoideus*)

The great bulk of the shoulder is formed by the
deltoid. It is, as its name implies, the delta-

shaped muscle, its contour approximating that triangular figure. It arises from the outer third of
the clavicle, and from the scapula. On this latter
bone it comes from its acromion process and the
lower lip of its spine. The coarse fibres, more or

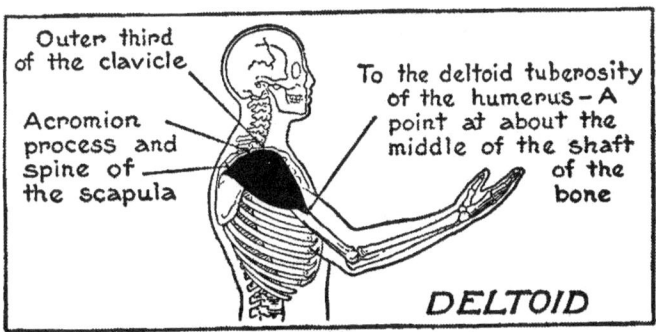

less in three divisions, converge toward the insertion into the humerus. The place of this insertion
—the deltoid tuberosity—is situated on the outer
surface at a point nearly to the middle of the shaft.
The coarseness of the fibres—a marked characteristic of this muscle—is often observable through the
integument.

The deltoid gives form to the shoulder and outlines from many points of view. The peculiarities
of the shoulder outlines in the two sexes are different. In the male the distinctive shape is such that
it helps to impart that squareness proper to an indi-

vidual of this sex.   But in the female the fulness is
below the summit of the shoulder; there is in this
case a somewhat gradual sloping from the neck over
the acromion to a bulging out—almost a sagging
effect, too—at the lower limit of the shoulder.
This contrasting difference in the contours of the
two shoulders should be particularly noticed in the
life class.

The deltoid is bordered on the back by the trapezius and the scapular muscles, and in front by the
greater pectoral.   The principal function of the
deltoid is to raise the arm to a position at right angles
with the trunk—or, perhaps, a little higher.   It co-
ordinates with the greater pectoral—which we study
next—in pulling the arm forward.

GREATER PECTORAL
(*Pectoralis major*)

This, the great muscle of the breast, covers the
front of the thorax from the clavicle to the level of
the fifth or sixth rib.   Its origins are from the inner half of the clavicle, the sternum, certain costal
cartilages, and by a fleshy slip from an aponeurosis
of an abdominal muscle.   Its free end is inserted
into the humerus on a ridge of the bicipital groove.
The greater pectoral is a thick layer of muscular
fibres, triangular in general outline, the apex the

insertion into the upper arm-bone, and the base the
border arising from the sternum. The narrowing
muscle twists immediately before reaching its insertion, so that the upper fibres go to a lower point
on the humerus, while the inferior fibres go to a

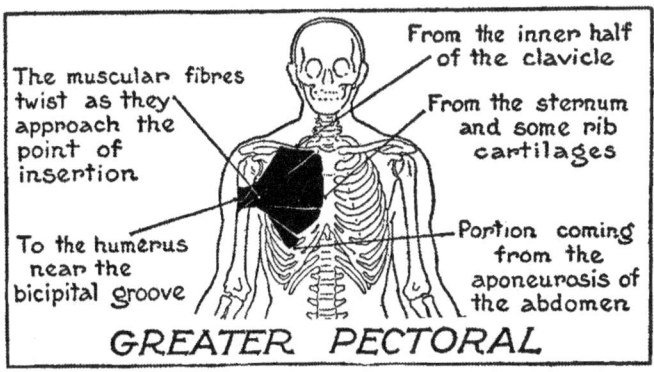

The muscular fibres twist as they approach the point of insertion.

From the inner half of the clavicle

From the sternum and some rib cartilages

To the humerus near the bicipital groove

Portion coming from the aponeurosis of the abdomen

GREATER PECTORAL

higher point on the bone. The central fibres find
their insertion at a midway point. (As we remember, the latissimus dorsi also twists its fibres as it
nears its insertion on the opposite, or inner, ridge of
the bicipital groove.)

As the greater pectoral is subcutaneous, its borders are clearly defined and its characteristics in
repose and movement are readily recognized. The
attention is called to a tiny triangular hollow that
marks an interval between the clavicular origin of
this muscle and that of the deltoid.

In very muscular models the lower border forms a nearly horizontal relief, and on the inner border, along the median line, where the fibres interlace with those of the opposite muscle, there is a depression. The breasts in the female, which lie over the fibres of this pectoral, are placed between the third and the sixth ribs. A matter that should be clearly understood when drawing the breasts in the female model is their position on the thorax; they are placed well over on the lateral regions toward the arms, and not in the very centres of the pectoral regions.

The greater pectoral draws the arm across the front of the trunk, and it also, as an antagonist to the deltoid and the upper part of the trapezius, pulls it down when it has been raised. When the arm is raised the lower part of the greater pectoral forms the anterior wall of the armpit. The position of the nipple, which in the male model shows on the inactive muscle between the fourth and fifth ribs, changes its position when the raised arm pulls on the fibres of the muscle.

When the arm is raised as high as it can be held, or in any great exertion or movement requiring such a position, this muscle will uncover a portion of a smaller pectoral form.

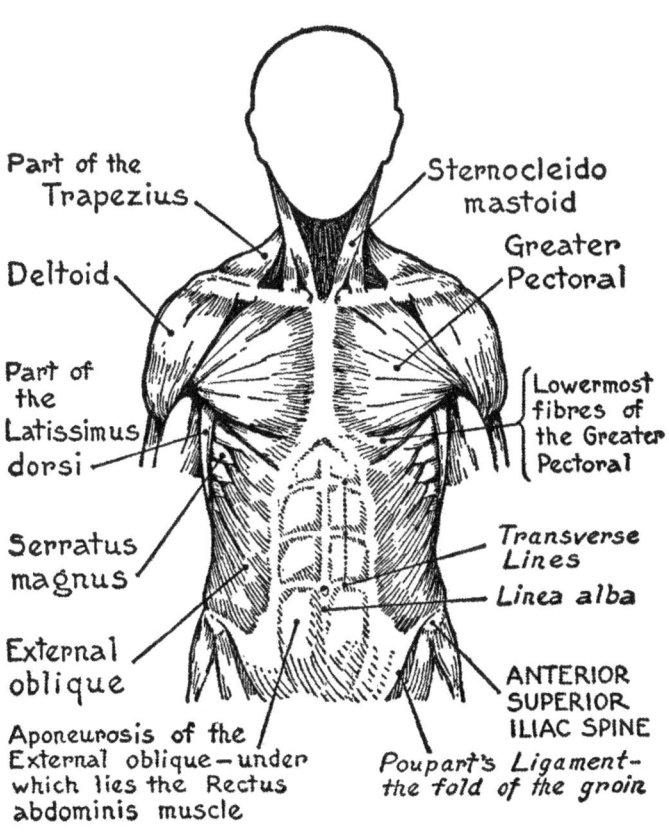

Part of the
Trapezius

Sternocleido
mastoid

Deltoid

Greater
Pectoral

Part of
the
Latissimus
dorsi

Lowermost
fibres of
the Greater
Pectoral

Serratus
magnus

Transverse
Lines

Linea alba

External
oblique

ANTERIOR
SUPERIOR
ILIAC SPINE

Aponeurosis of the
External oblique—under
which lies the Rectus
abdominis muscle

Poupart's Ligament-
the fold of the groin

THE MUSCLES OF THE FRONT OF THE TRUNK.

LESSER PECTORAL
(*Pectoralis minor*)

This muscle arises from the third, fourth, and fifth ribs by slips that converge to be inserted into the coracoid process—that beak-like formation of the scapula. Although it is covered by the greater

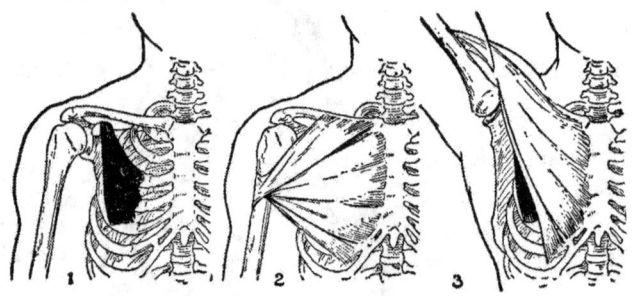

THE POSITION OF THE LESSER PECTORAL.

1. Its attachments.   2. The greater pectoral which covers it.   3. How a small portion becomes subcutaneous in the raising of the arm.

pectoral muscle, and has rarely any influence on the outer relief, except in the unusual case of raising the arm very high, as mentioned immediately above, it is included in our study on account of its functional activity. For instance, it pulls the shoulder down by its action on the scapula, and again, it pulls this bone around to glide over the thorax wall in the various movements of the shoulder.

SERRATUS MAGNUS
(*Serratus anterior*)

This muscle, belonging principally to the lateral region of the thorax, is of interest to us, as artists, for two reasons: firstly, on account of its fleshy slips, or digitations, that show so clearly as a row

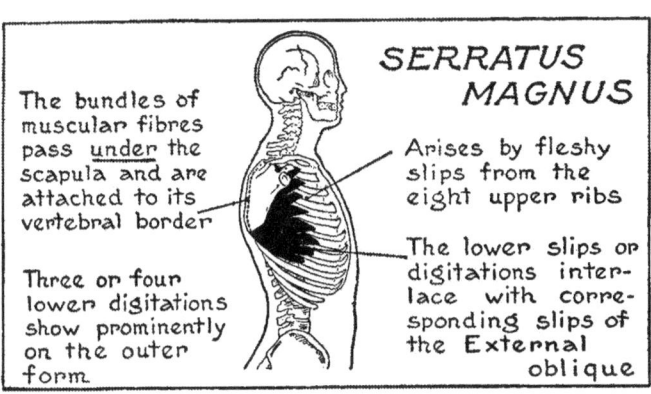

SERRATUS
MAGNUS

The bundles of muscular fibres pass <u>under</u> the scapula and are attached to its vertebral border

Three or four lower digitations show prominently on the outer form

Arises by fleshy slips from the eight upper ribs

The lower slips or digitations interlace with corresponding slips of the External oblique

of reliefs on the side of the thorax under the armpit; and, secondly, on account of its function in helping to hold the scapula close to the thorax, and moving it during movements of the shoulder and arm.

The serratus magnus arises by fleshy slips, or digitations, from the upper eight,—or nine,—ribs. These digitations converge as they pass around the side of the thorax to the posterior region, where they are attached along the vertebral border of the scapula. It is to be kept in mind that the muscle passes under the scapula. Its insertion is bordered by that of the rhomboid muscle. The two muscles are, in a way, by their continuity of fibres, one muscle, with the attached scapula as a

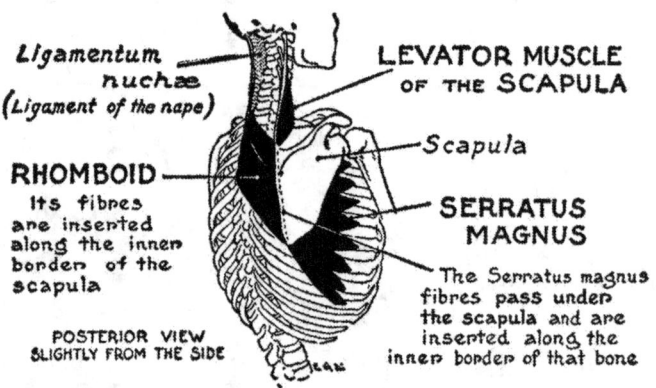

Ligamentum nuchae
(Ligament of the nape)

LEVATOR MUSCLE OF THE SCAPULA

Scapula

RHOMBOID
Its fibres are inserted along the inner border of the scapula

SERRATUS MAGNUS
The Serratus magnus fibres pass under the scapula and are inserted along the inner border of that bone

POSTERIOR VIEW SLIGHTLY FROM THE SIDE

THREE MUSCLES THAT ACT ON THE SCAPULA AND HELP TO HOLD IT IN PLACE.

bony transverse interval. But in the matter of function, they are quite antagonistic: the rhomboid pulls the scapula toward the middle line of the back, while the serratus magnus exerts its influence in a contrary direction, toward the front of the thorax.

This muscle is covered in part by the latissimus dorsi and the greater pectoral, its subcutaneous portion is that row of very perceptible reliefs below the outer lower margin of the breast muscle on the side of the thorax. These reliefs answer to four or five lower digitations—they dovetail in with, as you perhaps have noticed on the model, similar formations. They are those of the next muscle which we study.

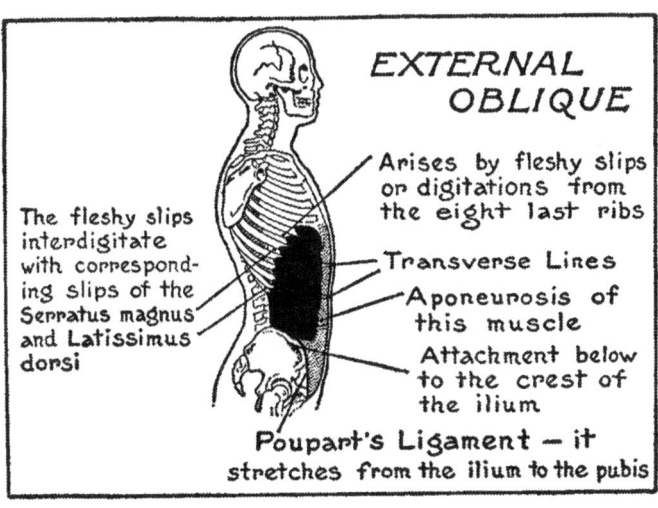

EXTERNAL OBLIQUE

Arises by fleshy slips or digitations from the eight last ribs

The fleshy slips interdigitate with corresponding slips of the Serratus magnus and Latissimus dorsi

Transverse Lines

Aponeurosis of this muscle

Attachment below to the crest of the ilium

Poupart's Ligament — it stretches from the ilium to the pubis

THE ABDOMEN AND THE FLANK

EXTERNAL OBLIQUE
(*Obliquus externus abdominis*)

This, the superficial muscular form of the abdomen, extends from the lower margin of the thorax to the lower part of the trunk, where it is separated from the thigh, at the groin, by the ligament of Poupart. Laterally its width is limited by the places of its insertion on the iliac crest and the eight lower ribs. The fleshy portion is found only in the flank, the abdominal part is entirely aponeurotic. Where the aponeurotic parts of the two muscles join on the middle line, the contiguous fibres interlace to form the linea alba, a dense white tissue stretching from the xiphoid process to the pubis at the middle of the figure.

The linea alba is crossed by irregular, or somewhat zigzagging, markings, called transverse lines. They correspond to certain tendinous intervals in the fibres of a muscle underlying the aponeurosis. The upper transverse line is slightly below the epigastric fossa (xiphoid process); a second is fixed at, or near, the level of the umbilicus, while a third is found midway between the two. Occasionally a fourth line appears below the umbilicus. These transverse lines are distinctive features of the region. In antique statuary they are very often indicated in a pattern-like, conventional way, rather than as they exist in the living model.

The origins of the external oblique from the lower ribs, besides interdigitating with some of the lower slips of the serratus magnus—as noted above—interlock on the flank, with three or four similar formations of the latissimus dorsi.

RECTUS ABDOMINIS

This is a long, straight muscle on the front of the abdomen, enclosed within a sheath composed of aponeuroses belonging to other muscles of the abdominal walls. The fleshy fibres extend from the

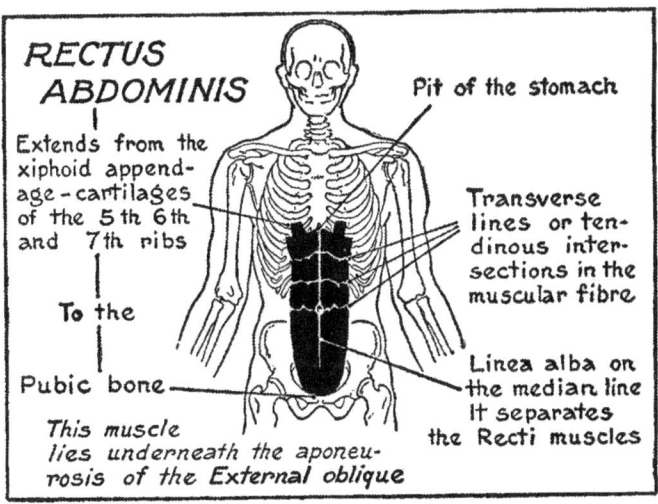

RECTUS ABDOMINIS

Extends from the xiphoid append-age - cartilages of the 5 th 6 th and 7 th ribs

To the

Pubic bone

This muscle lies underneath the aponeu-rosis of the External oblique

Pit of the stomach

Transverse lines or ten-dinous inter-sections in the muscular fibre

Linea alba on the median line It separates the Recti muscles

ziphoid process and some of the lower true ribs to the pubic bone. The linea alba divides the two recti muscles. The transverse lines in the superimposed aponeurosis of the external oblique answer to tendinous intersections in the fleshy fibres of the muscle.

The rectus abdominis is the only fleshy muscular

form on the abdomen, with the exception of a very small one, the pyramidalis, at the lower part.

The two recti muscles acting in concord are powerful flexors of the trunk. Again, they help by their fabric and with that of other muscles,

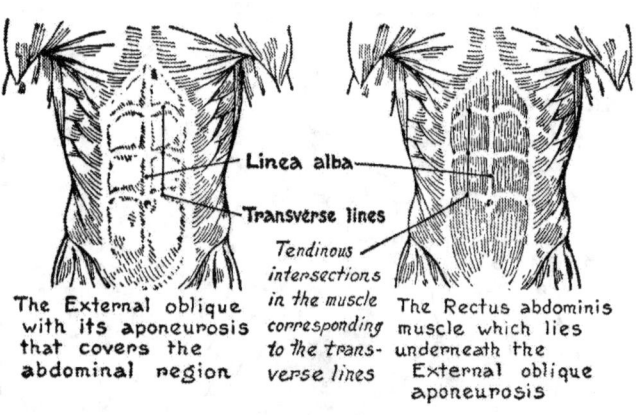

Linea alba

Transverse lines

Tendinous intersections in the muscle corresponding to the transverse lines

The External oblique with its aponeurosis that covers the abdominal region

The Rectus abdominis muscle which lies underneath the External oblique aponeurosis

TO SHOW THE LINEA ALBA AND THE TRANSVERSE LINES OF THE ABDOMINAL REGION.

to enclose the cavity of the abdomen. The bony thorax contains and protects the heart and lungs; but the organs of the lower region of the trunk, although held by the pelvic basin, depend mainly for protection and lateral support upon the surrounding muscular and aponeurotic walls. In this connection it will be worth while giving a few moments' attention to the anatomical peculiarities of these structures. There are two more of these muscular walls, besides those already mentioned. In the case of the INTERNAL OBLIQUE (*obliquus internus abdominis*), which extends from the crest of the ilium to the lower ribs, the fibres run, in general, obliquely and diametrically opposed to the

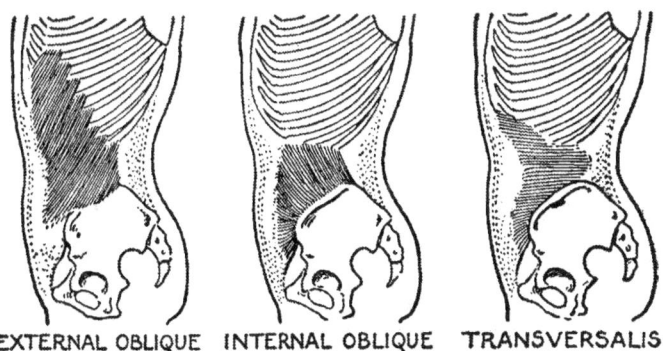

EXTERNAL OBLIQUE   INTERNAL OBLIQUE   TRANSVERSALIS

DIAGRAM TO ILLUSTRATE THE ANTAGONISTIC CHARACTER OF
THE FIBRES OF THREE MUSCLES OF THE ABDOMINAL WALLS.

direction of the fibres of the overlying muscle, the external oblique. In the next, the deepest layer, the TRANSVERSALIS (*transversus abdominis*), the fibres go horizontally, and are so opposed in their direction to both oblique muscles. This is an arrangement that gives strength to the lateral and anterior abdominal walls. The opposing fibres maintain the structure of the abdomen, but yield when the trunk is flexed.

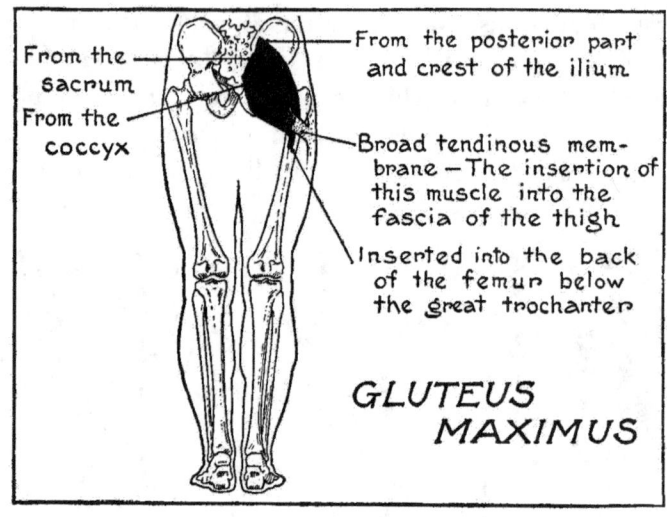

From the sacrum

From the coccyx

From the posterior part and crest of the ilium

Broad tendinous membrane — The insertion of this muscle into the fascia of the thigh

Inserted into the back of the femur below the great trochanter

GLUTEUS MAXIMUS

The Gluteal Region

GLUTEUS MAXIMUS

Both muscles of the gluteal region that we include in our study take origin from some part of the pelvic girdle and are inserted into the thighbone.

The gluteus maximus arises from the extreme posterior part of the ilium and parts of the sacrum and the coccyx. One tendon of insertion is attached to the posterior surface of the femur immediately below the great trochanter, and another by a broad tendinous membrane that blends with the fascia of the thigh. This gluteal muscle is large and thick, and roughly block-like in formation. It has the greater share in determining the form in the gluteal region. Fat, which is present to a great degree in this region, is often the chief factor in determining the form, however. It then masks the characteristic shape of the gluteal muscles. They take on, then, a rounded appearance instead of their characteristic formation. A depression should be noted on the lateral aspect of the region immediately back of the prominence of the great trochanter. This marks a tendinous expansion from the gluteus maximus muscle.

The gluteus maximus extends the thigh and pulls it back when it has been flexed. In addition, it is one of the muscles that maintains the body in the erect position, holding, when the legs are fixed, the trunk in place.

The line separating the gluteal region from the back of the thigh answers somewhat to the lower posterior border of the muscle. It is called the gluteal fold. In bending the trunk forward—that is, flexion—the fold disappears. In the relaxed muscle, on a limb that is not supporting the weight of the body, the fold takes an oblique direction, its outer end losing its form and blending with the general roundness of the thigh.

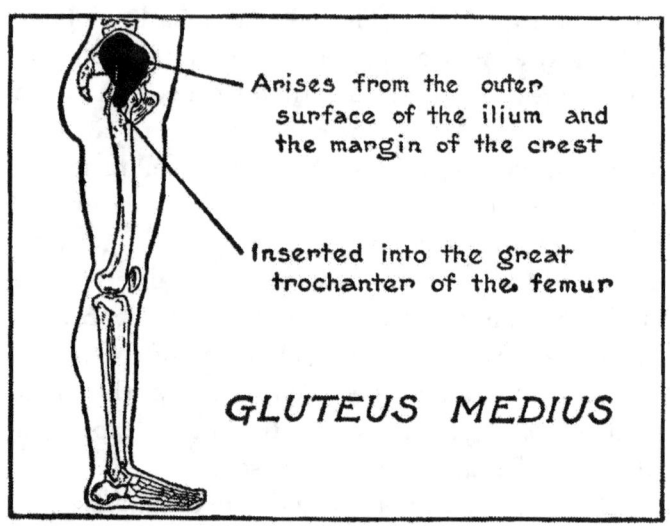

Arises from the outer
surface of the ilium and
the margin of the crest

Inserted into the great
trochanter of the femur

GLUTEUS MEDIUS

GLUTEUS MEDIUS

The gluteus medius, much smaller than the form just described, is situated on the forward part of the region. (The gluteus maximus, as we have stated, is the principal factor in the formation of the posterior gluteal region.) This small gluteus arises from about three-fourths of the posterior crest of the ilium, and the adjacent part of the fossa. It is inserted into the great trochanter of the femur. Its principal function, as we can see by this arrangement of its fibres, is to abduct the thigh. A supplementary function is that of a slight rotating of the thigh, and it helps, too, in keeping the trunk in its proper relationship with the lower limb in the erect position.

The gluteus medius is covered on its anterior part by a strong membranous sheet that blends with the fascial tendon of the gluteus maximus. This latter form also covers part of the gluteus medius. There is a deep-seated minor gluteal muscle (*gluteus minimus*) underlying these two principal ones. It helps to fill out the form in the region and co-ordinates with the other gluteals in function.

VIII

THE MUSCLES OF THE HEAD AND THE NECK

THE HEAD

WHEN we come to the study of the musculature of the head we find that there is a distinctive difference in their plan from that of the large structural muscles. Those that move the various segments of the jointed skeleton go, in nearly every case, from the surface of one bone to the surface of another. Now, with the exception of the muscles of mastication, the typical head muscle is one that has its origin on bone and its insertion into the integument. This method: a fixed point to bone and a free end into the skin is the characteristic plan of the cranial and facial muscles. To be sure, in some cases muscular margins and extremities blend with adjoining muscular parts.

(1) THE CRANIAL MUSCLE
OCCIPITO-FRONTALIS

This is the sole muscular tissue in the epicranial (upon the cranium) region. It covers the back and

top of the brain-box and the forehead. Its fixed
point to bone is at the occiput, where for a short
distance fleshy fibres are present, then follows the
thin aponeurotic sheet that extends over the cranium
to the upper border of the forehead, where again

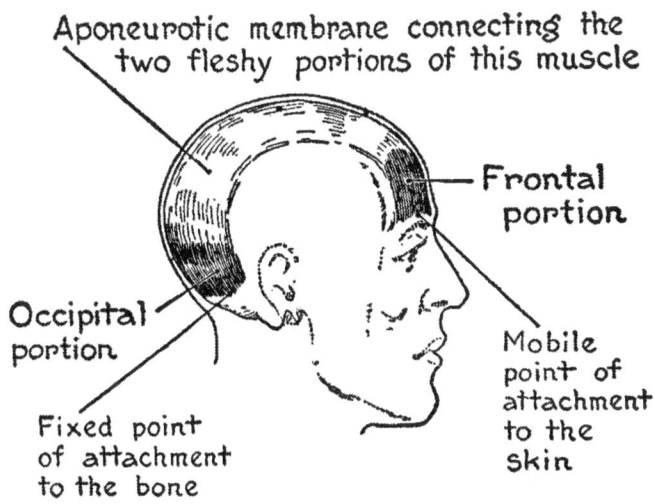

Aponeurotic membrane connecting the
    two fleshy portions of this muscle

Frontal
portion

Occipital
portion

Fixed point
of attachment
to the bone

Mobile
point of
attachment
to the
skin

OCCIPITO-FRONTALIS MUSCLE.

fleshy fibres appear. This latter portion is the free
end—that attached to the skin over the eyebrows.
    In action this muscle raises the eyebrows and
wrinkles the forehead horizontally, imparting an expression of surprise, or attention, to the features.
Sometimes the two portions of this muscle are dis-

tinguished as separate muscles: the anterior portion considered as the frontal, and the posterior portion as the occipital muscle. In this case they are thought of as tensors of the thin epicranial aponeurosis.

(2) THE MUSCLES OF EXPRESSION

The forms placed under this grouping can also be described as FACIAL MUSCLES.

ORBICULAR MUSCLE OF THE EYE
(*Orbicularis palpebrarum*)

This consists of a series of concentric fibrous rings around the eye. It is attached by a small division to the inner angle of the orbit. Fibres of the outer circumference blend or mingle with neighboring muscles. The inner rings, the palpebral part, correspond to the eyelids. It is this portion of the muscle that is in activity during the involuntary blinking of the eyes. In such movement as the sudden and forcible closing of the eye, that caused, for instance, by the avoidance of the glare of a blinding light, the whole muscle is in function. (Opening the eye by the lifting of the upper lid is effected by a special muscle, the levator muscle of the upper lid. It does not show outwardly, as it is entirely within the orbit.)

ORBICULAR MUSCLE OF THE MOUTH
(*Orbicularis oris*)

Another muscle of a circular form, but surrounding the mouth. Its function is, primarily, to close the mouth. The inner or labial fibres operate mainly, however, on the lips, while the outer rings blend their fibres with the free ends of other facial muscles. In this capacity it acts as the antagonist to the various muscles so attached. The muscle is joined in a few places, by slips of fibres, to the underlying bony surfaces.

CORRUGATOR OF THE EYEBROW
(*Corrugator supercilii*)

A small muscle situated on the upper border of the orbit close to the root of the nose, and placed under the frontalis muscle. Its attachment to bone is the inner part of the superciliary ridge, and its free end blends with the contiguous tissues. The right and left corrugators in action at the same time, pulling obliquely inward and downward, occasion the vertical furrows between the eyebrows, giving to the face an expression of grief, or pain.

PYRAMIDALIS NASI
(*Procerus*)

A slip of muscle at the root of the nose and which may be considered as an extension of the anterior part of the occipito-frontalis. It helps to pull the inner angles of the eyebrows downward, and causes short horizontal wrinkles at the root of the nose. A feature that adds emphasis to the expressions of anger and displeasure.

COMPRESSOR NARIS
(*Nasalis*)

This is a small muscle on the side of the nose, extending from its fixation on the upper maxilla to the middle line of the nose. Here its free fibres join with those of the opposite side. This muscle acts on the adjacent cartilaginous parts of the nose.

ELEVATOR OF THE UPPER LIP AND THE WING OF THE NOSE
(*Levator labii superioris alæque nasi*)

This muscle arises from the upper part of the superior maxillary bone, near the rim of the orbit, and passes downward to be inserted into the outer rings of the orbicular muscle of the mouth. At the wing of the nose a fibrous slip joins a cartilage of

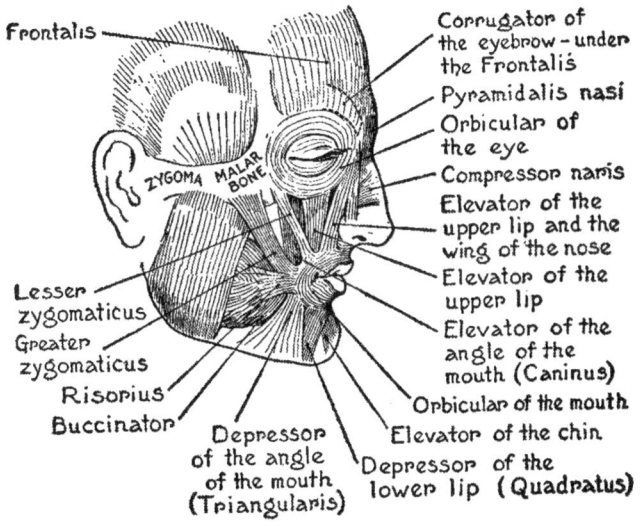

Frontalis

Corrugator of
the eyebrow – under
the Frontalis

Pyramidalis nasi

Orbicular of
the eye

Compressor naris

Elevator of the
upper lip and the
wing of the nose

Elevator of the
upper lip

Elevator of the
angle of the
mouth (Caninus)

Orbicular of the mouth

ZYGOMA MALAR BONE

Lesser
zygomaticus

Greater
zygomaticus

Risorius

Buccinator

Depressor
of the angle
of the mouth
(Triangularis)

Elevator of the chin

Depressor of the
lower lip (Quadratus)

THE MUSCLES OF EXPRESSION.

the region. The function of this muscle is made
sufficiently clear by its long name. When in action
its contracting fibres pull on the wing of the nose
and give a scornful curl to the upper lip.

ELEVATOR OF THE UPPER LIP
(Levator labii superioris proprius)

This, the special muscle that raises the upper lip,
is a form bordering and partly covered by the one
described immediately above. It is joined to the
bony surface close to the rim of the orbital cavity.

Its free end mingles with the muscular fibres around the mouth.

LESSER ZYGOMATICUS
(*Zygomaticus minor*)

A small strip of muscle placed over the elevator of the angle of the mouth (noted next). It is inserted into the orbicular fibres around the mouth. Its origin is from the fore part of the malar bone near the base of the zygomatic process.

ELEVATOR OF THE ANGLE OF THE MOUTH
(*Levator anguli oris*)
(*Caninus*)

The canine muscle, placed close to the elevator of the upper lip, arising from the superior maxillary bone below the orbit and joining, at the angle of the mouth, the fibres of the orbicularis. When in action the angle of the mouth is drawn upward. When functionating very strongly it opens the mouth slightly and exposes the canine tooth, giving a sneering look to the countenance.

GREATER ZYGOMATICUS
(*Zygomaticus major*)

This is generally considered as the muscle of laughter. It takes origin from the malar bone—its zygomatic process—from whence the fibres run obliquely to the corner of the mouth. Here they are inserted into the outer margin of the orbicular muscle. When in function the greater zygomaticus pulls the angle of the mouth upward and backward, puffs up the cheeks, and with the other conformable changes in the features, gives an expression of mirthfulness.

There is another muscle mentioned by anatomists as having a certain share in imparting a pleasing look to the face. It is a small slip of fibres called the RISORIUS of Santorini. This, the smiling muscle, is found on the cheek near the angle of the mouth. It is variable in form and particulars, and merely combines with other parts of the superficial musculature. It is a skin muscle, in fact, and is identified as an offshoot of the platysma, a muscular layer to be described further on.

ELEVATOR OF THE CHIN
(*Levator labii inferioris*)
(*Levator menti*)

Arises from the front of the lower jaw and extends downward only a short distance to its insertion into the integument. It pulls the chin up, causes wrinkles in the skin of the region, and gives to the countenance a look of doubt and aversion.

DEPRESSOR OF THE LOWER LIP
(Depressor labii inferioris)
(Quadratus menti)

A small square muscle that ascends from its origin on the bone to the orbicular fibres surrounding the mouth. The direction of the muscle as it goes upward tends toward the middle line of the chin, directly below the lips, where it meets the corresponding muscle of the opposite side. Its function, as its name indicates, is to pull down the lower lip.

DEPRESSOR OF THE ANGLE OF THE MOUTH
(Depressor anguli oris)
(Triangularis)

This is a muscle that participates to a very great extent in the play of the features. It arises from a line on the side of the lower jaw-bone near its inferior border. From this origin the muscle narrows and converges to be inserted into the angle of the mouth. This muscle, as can be seen by its position, depresses the angle of the mouth and lengthens the nasolabial furrow, that marked lineament starting at the wing of the nose and passing downward to the region of the angle of the mouth. This furrow and the fold of flesh that borders it on the cheek vary much in character, according to the individual or the expression. In smiling, for instance, it takes on a slight curve, and in laughter becomes strongly convex, or with a double-curving effect. When the angle of the mouth is strongly depressed by this muscle, the nasolabial furrow becomes severely straight and gives the face an expression depicting grief or melancholy.

BUCCINATOR

This is termed the cheek muscle, as its layer of fibres forms the wall of the mouth and constitutes part of the thickness of that region. The buccinator stretches between the two jaw-bones, the fibres being attached to their surfaces near the sockets of the back teeth. The anterior fibres go to be inserted into the angle of the mouth. As it is the chief factor in forcing the air out of the distended cheek in playing wind-instruments, the buccinator is called the trumpeter's muscle. It also aids in mastication by keeping the food between the back teeth while it is being crushed and ground by them.

(3) THE MUSCLES OF MASTICATION
MASSETER AND TEMPORAL

Of the muscles of mastication, only two—named above—take any part in the superficial anatomy of the head. In nearly all of the facial muscles we saw that the characteristic thing about them is that they are joined by one end to a bony surface, and by the other to some soft and easily moved tissue, like the skin, or some other muscle. Now the two muscles of the head which we are going to consider here extend their fibres from the surface of

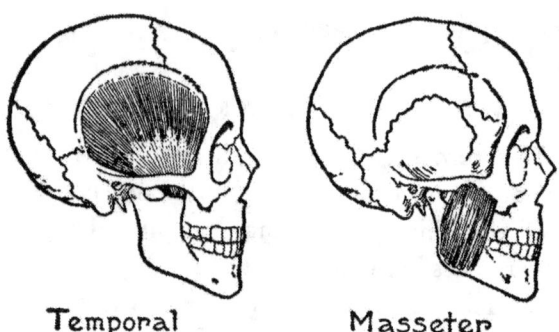

Temporal   Masseter

TWO MUSCLES OF MASTICATION.

one bone to that of another; or, particularizing a little further, take origin on the theoretically stationary skull, to be affixed to the movable lower jawbone.

The masseter is placed at the back part of the cheek, where it arises from the zygomatic arch to be inserted into the inferior maxillary bone along its lower edge, angle, and the surface of the ascending branch, or ramus. Its principal function, as the arrangement of the fibres clearly indicate, is to raise the lower jaw.

The second muscle, the temporal, also raises the lower jaw. It comes from the side of the cranium in the temporal fossa, or that region nearly corresponding to the temples. Its converging fibres descend to pass under the zygomatic arch to their insertion into the coronoid process of the lower jawbone. The contracting and relaxing fibres, as they alternate in movement, can be observed on the side of the temple when the muscle is put into action.

THE NECK

The whole region of the back of the neck is covered by the superior portion of the trapezius muscle. This form also extends, as we have learned, somewhat toward the anterior region. As the trapezius has been described, we go on now to the consideration of the other muscles of the neck.

(1) THE MUSCLES OF THE SIDE AND THE POSTERIOR REGION OF THE NECK

STERNOCLEIDOMASTOID
(Sternocleidomastoideus)

We take note, first, of this important detail of the region. It is a very long muscle with a very long name. It is a cord-like band that goes from the top of the sternum obliquely across the neck to the

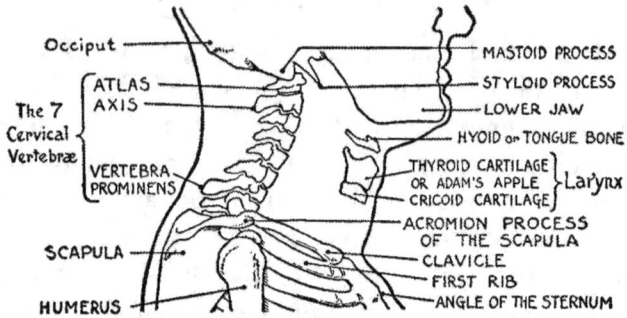

THE BONES OF THE NECK, INCLUDING THE TONGUE–BONE AND
THE LARYNX.

head, directly back of the ear. At the top of the
sternum between the origins of the two muscles is
that conspicuous depression—precedently mentioned
—called the fonticulus, or the pit of the neck.

This muscle is a determining feature in studying

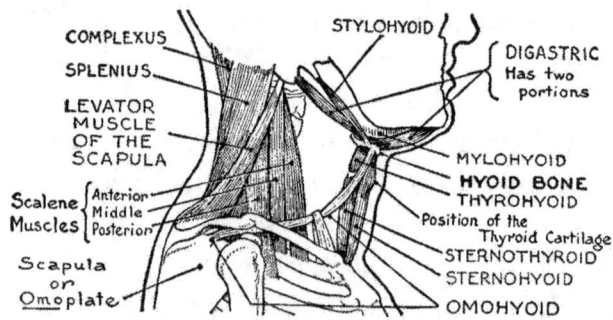

DEEP MUSCLES OF THE POSTERIOR REGION OF THE NECK AND
THE THROAT MUSCLES. NOTE ESPECIALLY THE DIRECTION
OF THE OMOHYOID.

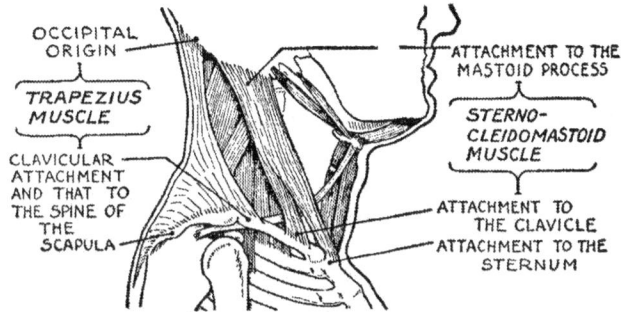

DIAGRAM TO SHOW THE SUBCUTANEOUS PARTS OF THE DEEP
NECK MUSCLES AND HOW THEY ARE COVERED BY THE
UPPER PORTION OF THE TRAPEZIUS AND THE STERNO-
CLEIDOMASTOID.

the anatomical details of the region. By it we fix
the positions of other anatomical parts of the region, and it is clearly seen, too, that it is in no less
degree a determining landmark in drawing. There

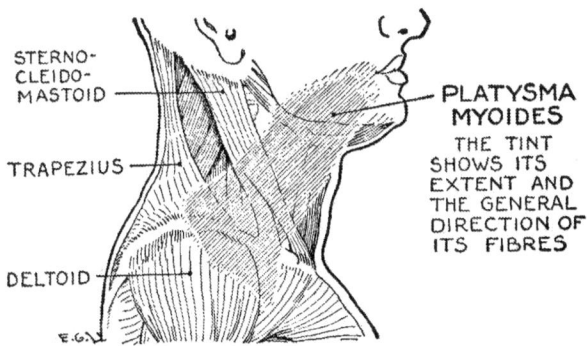

DIAGRAM TO SHOW THE POSITION OF THE THIN SHEET OF
MUSCULAR FIBRES CALLED THE PLATYSMA MYOIDES.

rarely is a model that does not show its form, more or less, clearly.

Although its name is long and awkward, it is quite the proper term to use, as its etymological divisions explain the attachments to bone: *sterno*, in reference to the origin from the sternum; *cleido*, having to do with its smaller origin from the clavicle (*cleido*, the Greek equivalent for the Latin *clavicula*); and *mastoid*, pertaining to the insertion into the mastoid process on the skull. It should be remarked in addition that a few fibres at the insertion go to the adjacent occipital bone.

Between the two origins—sternal and clavicular—there is an interval which sometimes marks a depression on the outer surface.

The sternocleidomastoid muscle turns the head away from the side of the particular muscle in action. It also inclines the head; when doing so, moves it toward the shoulder of the side of the muscle which is functionating. In general the two muscles are antagonistic. The two muscles, though, when they act together depress the head.

There is frequently observable in lean persons a swollen line crossing this muscle. It is the superficial course of the external jugular vein, that arises by the union of smaller veins on the side of the neck, near the angle of the lower jaw. When the vein has crossed the sternocleidomastoid, it dips into the trunk in the region immediately above the middle of the clavicle. This vein in expressions of rage and passion is usually much dilated, and very conspicuous.

Between the long line of the sternocleidomastoid and the anterior margin of the superior part of the trapezius is a triangular area. The edges of the two muscles constitute the sides, and the converging edges at the skull the apex of this triangle. The base is the middle portion of the clavicle. There may be, unless there is a mass of fat to fill it up, a depression at the base of this area, immediately above the clavicle. Often, though, there is an unmistakable hollow that brings out in strong relief the shaft of the clavicle. An observation should be made here with respect to the clavicular insertion of the trapezius; its usual attachment is only to the outer third of the bone, leaving an interval between it and the clavicular origin of the sternocleidomastoid. But sometimes this trapezius insertion has its fibres reaching nearly to the other muscular part. This has an important bearing on the outer formation of the neck and shoulders, because in such a case the depression we have spoken of is absent or but slightly perceptible.

COMPLEXUS
(*Semispinalis capitus*)

SPLENIUS
(*Splenius capitus*)

Within the triangular area defined above, five muscles of the neck sometimes disclose portions of their fibres subcutaneously. The two that we now consider, act on the skull, balanced as it is on the top of the spinal column. They also co-ordinate with other muscles to extend or pull it back.

The complexus reaches from the four lower cervical and some dorsal vertebræ to the skull, there to be inserted into the occipital bone. The complexus is covered in part by the splenius, which muscle goes from the seventh cervical and some upper dorsal vertebræ to the skull. There it is attached to the occipital bone and the mastoid process of the temporal bone.

LEVATOR MUSCLE OF THE SCAPULA
(*Levator anguli scapulæ*)

This in the region of the neck borders the splenius. It is not attached to the skull, however, but arises from the transverse processes of the three, or four, cervical vertebræ. From here they stretch to the inner superior angle of the scapula. The levator muscle of the scapula co-ordinates with two other muscles—already noted—that are attached to the scapula; namely, the rhomboid and the serratus magnus. (See page 144.)

SCALENE MUSCLES
(Scalenus anterior, medius, and posterior)

This is a group of three fleshy strips that pass from the processes of six cervical (second to seventh) vertebræ to the skeleton of the thorax. Here they are joined to the first two ribs. Their subcutaneous portions proceed across the triangular area above the clavicle.

The scalene muscles, when the vertebral attachments are the fixed points, lift the ribs. They are considered then as respiratory muscles. If, when taking a deep breath, you make a special effort to lift the upper part of the thorax, their forms can be felt becoming tense and firm.

The greater part of the four muscular divisions described immediately above are covered by the superficial trapezius and the sternocleidomastoid muscles.

(2) THE MUSCLES OF THE THROAT

The fifth muscle that shows part of its length within the triangular space on the side of the neck is one of the throat muscles, the OMOHYOID. This is a ribbon of fleshy and tendinous fibres that has

rather a curious trend between its two attachments
—one the scapular region and the other the throat.

The omohyoid arises from the upper margin of
the scapula, is directed forward on the side of the
neck, then passes under the sternocleidomastoid,
where it turns suddenly at an angle upward to the
tongue-bone. At the angle where it changes its
course it is held in place by a loop of fascial tissue.
This slender muscle sometimes shows, in certain
phases of activity, in persons with necks sparsely
covered by flesh.

When the throat is looked at directly from the
front and considered merely diagrammatically, the
aspect, as it presents itself to the eye, is that of an
inverted triangle. The apex at the pit of the neck,
the up-turned base corresponding to the level of
the jaw-bone, and the sides formed by the borders
of the two sternocleidomastoid muscles. Within this
area are found the throat muscles; the hyoid, or
tongue-bone; and the organ of the voice, or the
larynx. By its bulk the larynx is an important
structure in the matter of filling out the form. The
throat muscles themselves are small and slender,
and rarely separately distinguishable, excepting the
omohyoid, which we have mentioned.

The part of the larynx that interests us in the
matter of making itself evident as an outer influence
on the form is the prominence of the thyroid car-

tilage, commonly termed the Adam's apple. This prominence juts out very strongly in the male, but rarely very much in the female, throat.

Briefly, the muscles of the throat coming close to the integument are:

The STERNOHYOID, going from the sternum to the tongue-bone. The STERNOTHYROID, also from the sternum, but going to the thyroid cartilage. The prolongation of this latter muscle is the THYROHYOID, continuing the form to the tongue-bone. These muscles, with the omohyoid, draw down the larynx and the hyoid bone.

The following act on the tongue-bone, draw it up, or hold it in place:

The STYLOHYOID, extending from a pointed projection of the temporal bone to the tongue-bone. The DIGASTRIC, extending from the temporal bone to the tongue-bone, where it is tendinous and held to the bone by a fibrous band. It continues by fleshy fibres to the inside of the jaw-bone directly back of the front of the chin. The MYLOHYOID, stretching between the lower jaw-bone and the tongue-bone.

The two mylohyoid muscles form the principal structure of the floor of the mouth. Some of the throat muscles pull down the lower jaw-bone in opening the mouth. It should be remembered, however, that the weight of the bone has some share in this action.

(3) The Superficial Muscle of the Neck and the Side of the Face

PLATYSMA

(Platysma myoides)

With the study of this anatomical item we conclude the study of the region to which this chapter has been devoted. The platysma is a very thin layer of fibre covering the side of the neck and extending upward to the cheek. Beginning below in the upper part of the chest and shoulders, it spreads over the side of the neck and continues to the face as far as the angle of the mouth and the front of the chin. In this region it blends its fibres with some facial muscles and other adjoining tissues. The risorius (precedently noted) is practically a small division of this muscle.

In its essential nature the platysma is a skin muscle, as it lies close under this membrane. In extending over the region it conforms to the relief of any part it crosses, as it is not in itself of thick enough texture to influence the general form.

The platysma draws down—as a co-ordinating factor in connection with other muscles—the angle of the mouth in expressions of terror. It causes, in some movements, on the side of the neck long, tense lines that go in the direction of its fibres. Or, again, in extreme terror, when, besides drawing down the corners of the mouth, the head is pulled over toward the shoulder, transverse wrinkles appear in the contracted integument of the region.

In either of the above cases—transverse wrinkles or long lines—the effect is unpleasant and conveys very forcibly the ideas of fright, terror, or similar displeasing expressions.

IX

THE MUSCLES OF THE UPPER LIMB

The Upper Arm

BEFORE going on with the description of the muscles of the upper limb, we will give a little attention to its general form. First of all it will be well to mention as a reminder that the usual anatomical diagrams of the arms, whether the views are anterior, posterior, or lateral, are drawn from limbs that are held in the position of supination. As we know, this position is that in which the forearm bones are parallel and the palm faces the front.

Now, with the arm held supinated, there is a peculiarity in relative shapes of the upper arm and the forearm that should be especially noted. Both the upper arm and the forearm in their transverse sections show that their respective bodies are somewhat elliptical. But the two divisions of the arm, with their elliptical bodies, are set one to the other with their respective major axes in opposition. Or, to explain the contrasting characteristics in the two parts of the limb in another way: in the limb when

176

looked at from the front, the upper arm looks narrow, while the forearm appears wider; and in the lateral view it is the upper arm that is widest, while the forearm is the narrowest.

Supination and pronation have been explained in

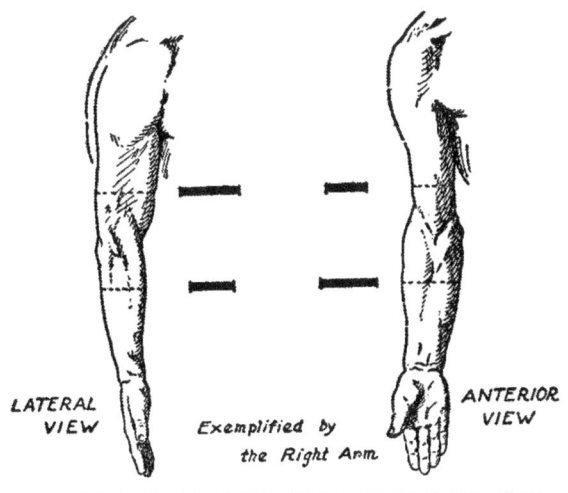

LATERAL VIEW   *Exemplified by the Right Arm*   ANTERIOR VIEW

DIAMETERS OF THE UPPER ARM AND OF THE FOREARM
COMPARED.

another chapter, but the effect of these movements on the musculature was not touched upon. With the arm supinated, the relative shapes of the muscles of the forearm are, in studying them from a diagram, readily perceptible and understood, but as soon as we begin to pronate the arm, uncertainty begins. By trying it yourself you can see how the

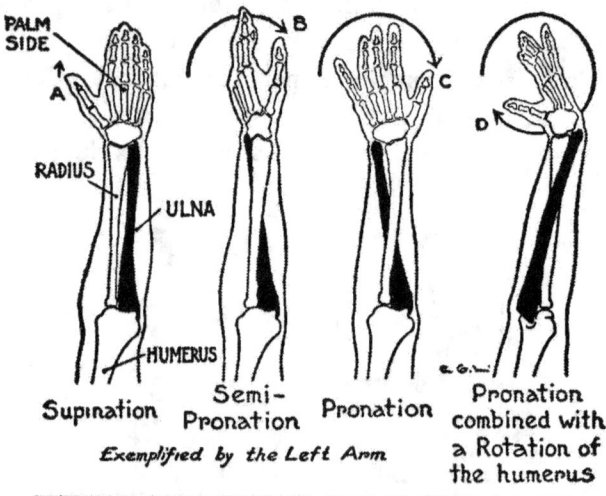

PALM SIDE
A
B
RADIUS
ULNA
C
D
HUMERUS

Supination   Semi-Pronation   Pronation   Pronation combined with a Rotation of the humerus

Exemplified by the Left Arm

EXTENT TO WHICH THE HAND CAN BE TURNED AND THE
THUMB MADE TO DESCRIBE NEARLY
A COMPLETE CIRCLE.

muscles begin to twist, as it were, in following the forearm in its pronation. By this practical experiment you can see, too, the degree to which the arm can be pronated and rotated. The thumb, for example, nearly describes a complete circle.

BICEPS OF THE ARM
(*Biceps flexor cubiti*)
(*Biceps brachii*)

The most characteristic and easiest recognized form of the arm. What changes take place in its conformation are simple ones; either it becomes

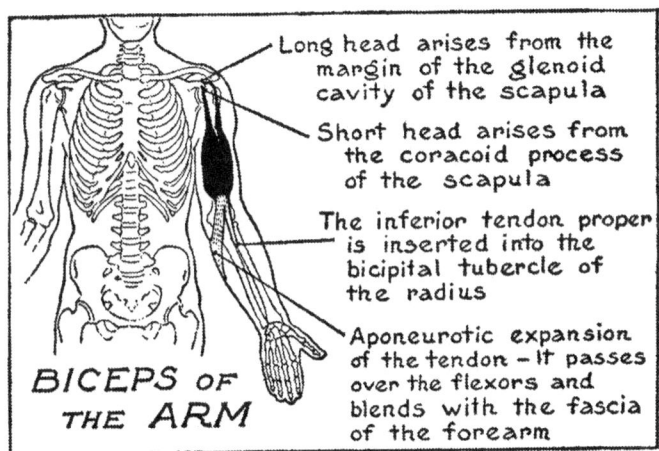

Long head arises from the margin of the glenoid cavity of the scapula

Short head arises from the coracoid process of the scapula

The inferior tendon proper is inserted into the bicipital tubercle of the radius

Aponeurotic expansion of the tendon – It passes over the flexors and blends with the fascia of the forearm

BICEPS OF THE ARM

more or less globular in contraction, or elongated in relaxing. The biceps arises from two places on the scapula. One is by a short head from the cora-coid process, and the other a long head from the margin of the glenoid cavity. These two heads, tendinous at their origins, unite to form the large mass of the muscle that we see on the front of the upper arm. The insertions are two: one to the radius by a tendon, and the other an aponeurotic expansion that blends with the fascia that covers the forearm. The biceps bends the elbow and flexes the forearm on the upper arm. By the peculiarity of its insertion into an inner point on the radius, it takes part in supination. This function can be demonstrated by bending the arm nearly at a right

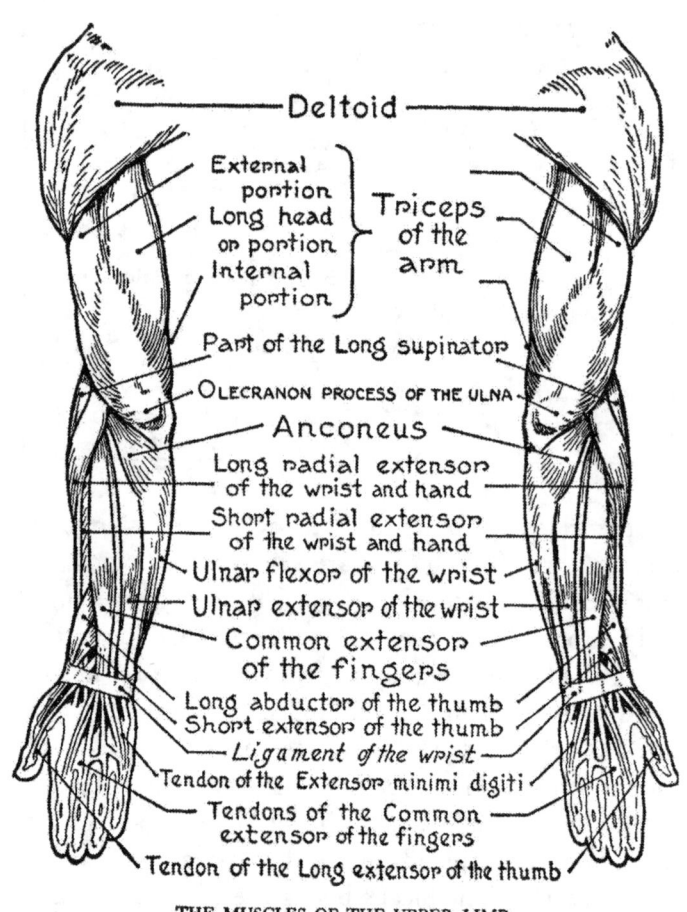

Deltoid

External portion
Long head or portion   Triceps of the arm
Internal portion

Part of the Long supinator

Olecranon process of the ulna

Anconeus

Long radial extensor of the wrist and hand

Short radial extensor of the wrist and hand

Ulnar flexor of the wrist

Ulnar extensor of the wrist

Common extensor of the fingers

Long abductor of the thumb

Short extensor of the thumb

Ligament of the wrist

Tendon of the Extensor minimi digiti

Tendons of the Common extensor of the fingers

Tendon of the Long extensor of the thumb

THE MUSCLES OF THE UPPER LIMB.
Posterior view.

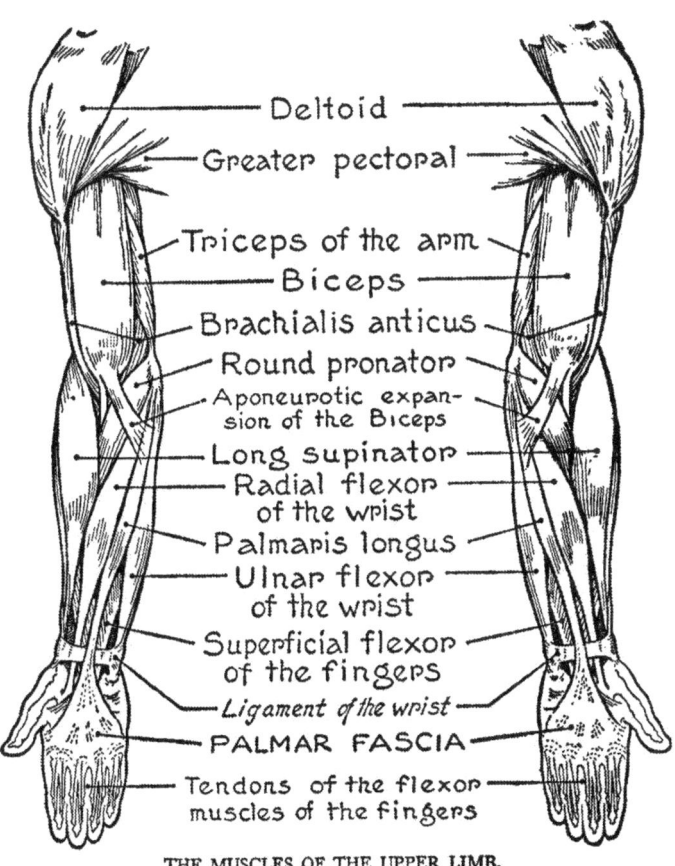

Deltoid

Greater pectoral

Triceps of the arm

Biceps

Brachialis anticus

Round pronator

Aponeurotic expansion of the Biceps

Long supinator

Radial flexor of the wrist

Palmaris longus

Ulnar flexor of the wrist

Superficial flexor of the fingers

Ligament of the wrist

PALMAR FASCIA

Tendons of the flexor muscles of the fingers

THE MUSCLES OF THE UPPER LIMB.
Anterior view.

angle, and then turning the hand in and out. Then the muscle plainly can be seen swelling out and relaxing by turns.

The large mass of the biceps, so definite in shape, gives unmistakable forms and contours. At the front of the elbow the aponeurotic expansion should be observed as it binds down and creates a shallow furrow across the inner forearm, while the tendon should be remarked as it dips into the pit of the elbow. Its special antagonist is the triceps.

TRICEPS OF THE ARM
(*Triceps extensor cubiti*)
(*Triceps brachii*)

A large muscle forming the whole region of the back of the upper arm. It arises from three places. One origin, the long head, comes from the scapula below the margin of the glenoid cavity. The other origins are from the humerus; of these, an external portion arises from the back of the humerus below the great tuberosity and an internal portion from the back and inner border of the bone. All three portions join a common tendon that is fixed to the ulna at the point of the elbow—that is to the olecranon process.

The general mass of the triceps gives the contours of the back of the upper arm, and its inner

and outer sides.   An important surface marking of
the triceps is the somewhat flattened space above
the olecranon.   This is caused by the plane of the
common tendon.   Such tendons, when large or ex-

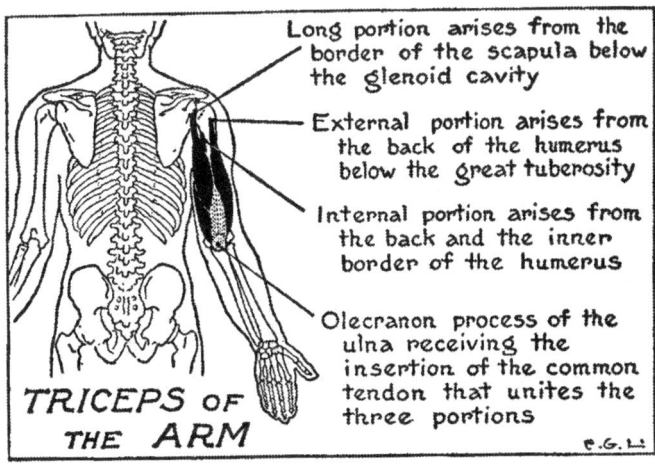

Long portion arises from the
border of the scapula below
the glenoid cavity

External portion arises from
the back of the humerus
below the great tuberosity

Internal portion arises from
the back and the inner
border of the humerus

Olecranon process of the
ulna receiving the
insertion of the common
tendon that unites the
three portions

TRICEPS OF
THE ARM

e.G.L.

panded, give in general, where they occur, broad
areas with very slight convexity.   Then where fleshy
fibres issue from such flattened tendinous portions
there is usually a discernible relief when a muscle
is well developed.

The triceps straightens out the flexed arm, and
is, as we have remarked above, the antagonist to
the biceps.

BRACHIALIS ANTICUS

This is a thick muscle stretching like a broad band across the anterior region of the elbow, from the humerus to the ulna. Its humeral origin is from the front of the bone and its adjacent inner

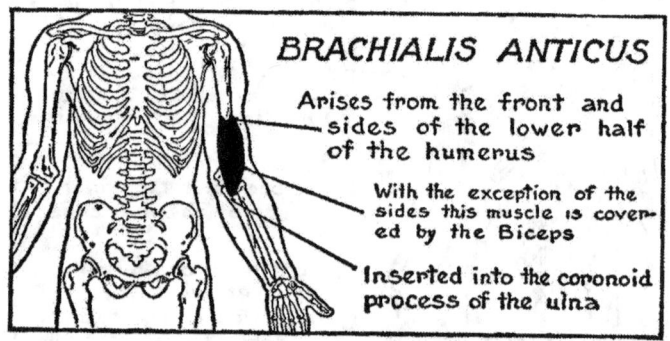

BRACHIALIS ANTICUS

Arises from the front and sides of the lower half of the humerus

With the exception of the sides this muscle is covered by the Biceps

Inserted into the coronoid process of the ulna

and outer borders. The insertion is on the ulna into its coronoid process, an eminence of the bone in front of the semilunar notch, which notch takes part in formation of the elbow-joint. The brachialis anticus is a direct flexor of the forearm on the upper arm. As it is covered in front by the mass of the biceps, it only presents its lateral borders subcutaneously, where they have, compared to the roundnesses produced by the biceps and triceps, but little influence on the outer relief.

CORACO-BRACHIALIS

This is a small muscle of simple form arising from the coracoid process of the scapula. (It is the last of the three muscles referred to as being attached

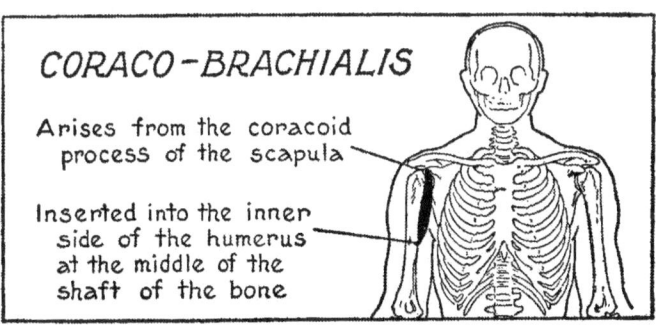

CORACO-BRACHIALIS

Arises from the coracoid
  process of the scapula

Inserted into the inner
  side of the humerus
  at the middle of the
  shaft of the bone

here; the other two are the lesser pectoral, and the biceps, by its short tendon.)

The coraco-brachialis goes to the humerus, and is inserted at about the middle of the shaft. Part of its fibres only are subcutaneous, and only when the arm is held up so as to expose the armpit. Then the narrow relief of the muscle can be observed coming out of the depth of the axilla and passing into the bulk of the arm between the adjoining borders of the biceps and the triceps. This muscle adducts the arm; that is, draws it toward the side of the body.

With this form, the coraco-brachialis, we complete
the simply planned muscular system of the upper
arm. The anatomy of the forearm, on the other
hand, is not so simple; it is a very much divided

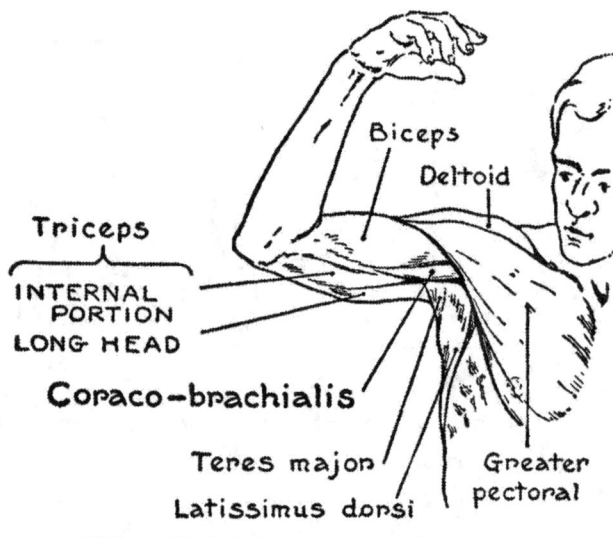

Biceps

Deltoid

Triceps

INTERNAL
PORTION
LONG HEAD

Coraco-brachialis

Teres major

Latissimus dorsi

Greater
pectoral

THE MUSCLES IN THE REGION OF THE AXILLA.

system of long muscles and tendons. Nearly all
the muscles of the forearm take their origins, or
some parts of their origins, from the upper arm-
bone. One of them, for example, arises from the
humerus at about the middle of the shaft. It is
the next muscle that we study.

THE FOREARM AND THE HAND

LONG SUPINATOR
(Supinator longus)
(Brachio-radialis)

This muscle with four other forearm muscles, to which we are going to direct our attention presently,

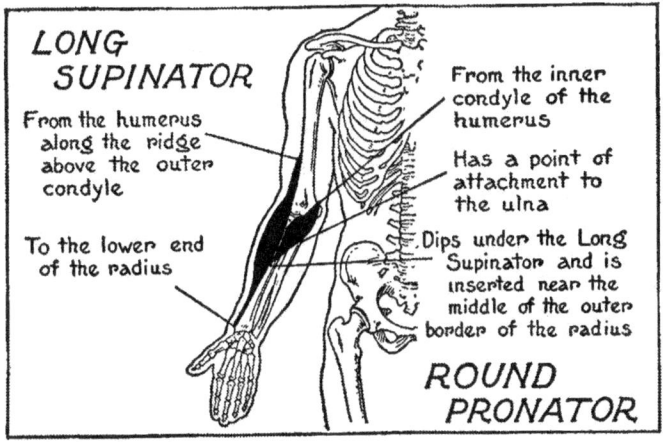

LONG
SUPINATOR

From the humerus along the ridge above the outer condyle

To the lower end of the radius

From the inner condyle of the humerus

Has a point of attachment to the ulna

Dips under the Long Supinator and is inserted near the middle of the outer border of the radius

ROUND
PRONATOR

arise on the humerus from its external condyle, or the lateral ridge above it. When we have deliberated upon them, we will turn our attention to those of another group that arise from the other condyle of the humerus, the inner, or medial, one.

It is a great help in remembering the muscular forms, their names, positions, and functions if we keep in mind the group to which a form belongs. And a good way, too, of working is to observe the muscular forms on your own arm by holding it out before you—with the book close at hand—and trying to find any particular muscle in question.

The long supinator lies on the external, or lateral, region of the arm; extending from its origin on the condylar ridge of the humerus to the end of the radius at the wrist. There it is inserted into the outer side of the bone. It is a long muscle, the lower third, or so, a tendon, and the middle a rather large fleshy portion forming some of the mass on the outer side of the upper third of the forearm. The origin is a flat band of fibres. The outer wall of the depression at the bend of the elbow—pit of the elbow—is formed by the body of the long supinator.

To bring out the muscle plainly, bend the arm to a right angle and hold a heavy weight in the hand, then the muscle will stand out clearly from the adjacent forms. It can be still better brought out into prominence by depending the weight from a cord held in the hand, or by placing the hand under the edge of some heavy piece of furniture, like a library-table, and trying to lift it. In the matter of function the long supinator is as much of a flexor of the arm as it is a supinator.

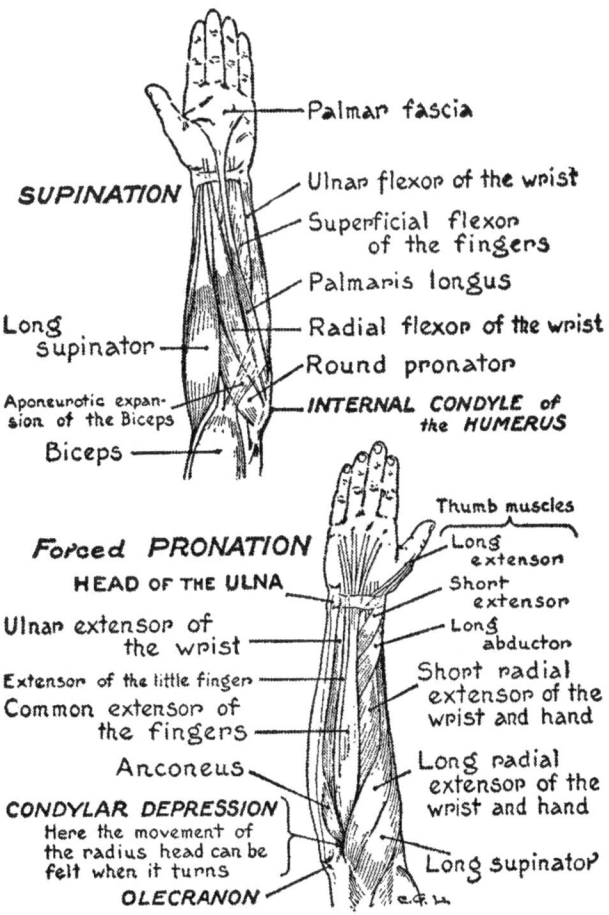

SUPINATION

Palmar fascia

Ulnar flexor of the wrist

Superficial flexor of the fingers

Palmaris longus

Radial flexor of the wrist

Long supinator

Round pronator

INTERNAL CONDYLE of the HUMERUS

Aponeurotic expansion of the Biceps

Biceps

Forced PRONATION

Thumb muscles

Long extensor

Short extensor

HEAD OF THE ULNA

Ulnar extensor of the wrist

Long abductor

Extensor of the little finger

Short radial extensor of the wrist and hand

Common extensor of the fingers

Anconeus

Long radial extensor of the wrist and hand

CONDYLAR DEPRESSION
Here the movement of the radius head can be felt when it turns

Long supinator

OLECRANON

With this diagram before you the muscles in your own forearm can be identified and studied.

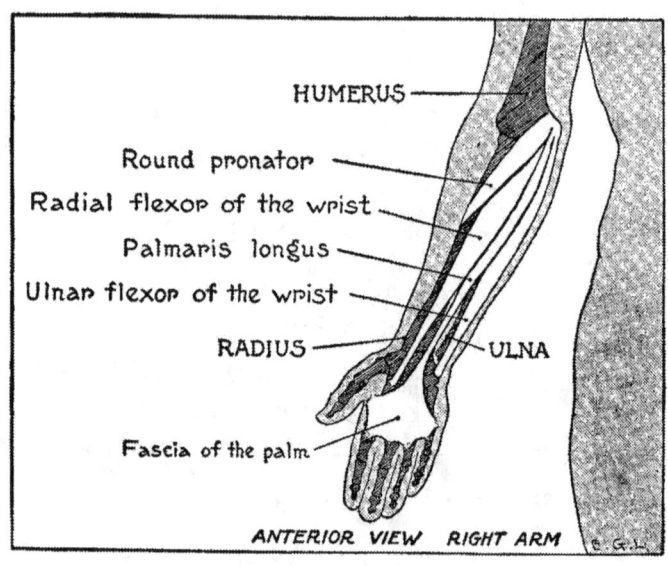

FOUR FOREARM MUSCLES THAT ARISE FROM THE INTERNAL
CONDYLE OF THE HUMERUS.

Now, passing around toward the posterior region of the forearm we come to the rest of the muscles arising from the external region of the humerus. They are all extensors of the wrist and hand, or of the fingers. A simple way of remembering from which side of the humerus these extensors arise is to keep before the mental vision the identity of the first four letters in both terms; then we will not forget that the *exte*nsors arise from the *exte*rnal side.

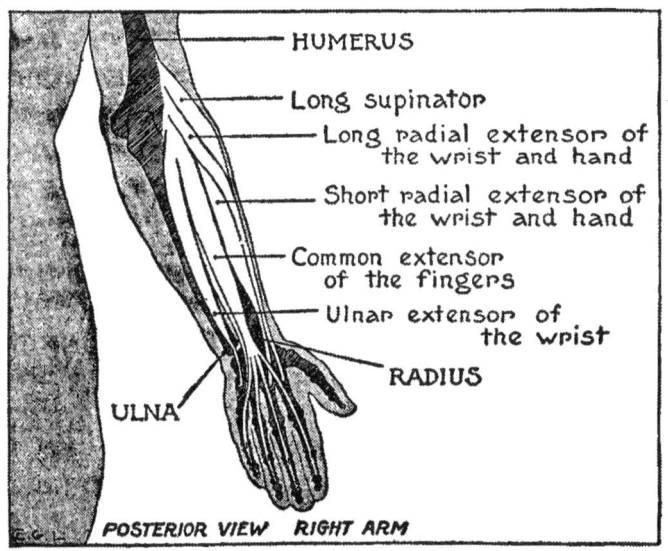

Labels on the figure:

HUMERUS

Long supinator

Long radial extensor of the wrist and hand

Short radial extensor of the wrist and hand

Common extensor of the fingers

Ulnar extensor of the wrist

RADIUS

ULNA

POSTERIOR VIEW   RIGHT ARM

FIVE FOREARM MUSCLES THAT ARISE FROM THE EXTERNAL
CONDYLE AND ADJACENT RIDGE OF THE HUMERUS.

LONG RADIAL EXTENSOR OF THE WRIST AND HAND
(*Extensor carpi radialis longior*)

This muscle arises from the humerus on its external ridge below the origin of the long supinator, which muscle it borders as it passes down the forearm, keeping, though, to the posterior side of the forearm. The fleshy portion ends at the middle of the forearm where the slender tendon begins to continue to the insertion into the second metacarpal bone, or that of the index-finger.

We noted how the long supinator formed the outer wall of the pit of the elbow. Now the long radial extensor of the wrist and hand borders the long supinator, and with it forms that obliquely running mass crossing the outer region of the elbow.

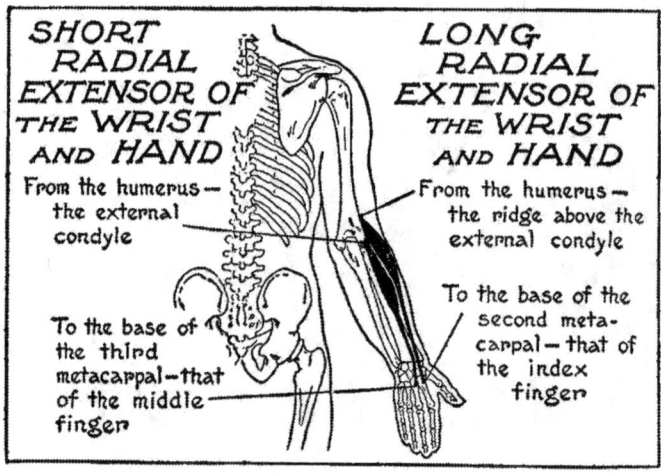

This mass is a distinguishing feature of the region to consider in drawing; it gives shapeliness and softens the outline of the various positions incident to the bending of the elbow. In extreme flexion, when the arm-bones are made to approach each other, this fleshy mass assumes other shapes, it is forced outwardly by the nearing bones, and instead of a depression on the front of the elbow, there is a crease.

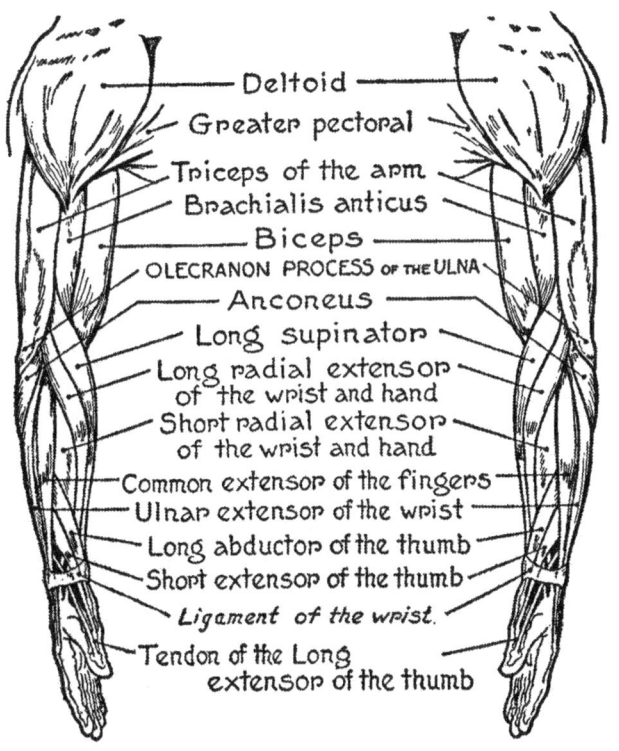

Deltoid

Greater pectoral

Triceps of the arm

Brachialis anticus

Biceps

OLECRANON PROCESS OF THE ULNA

Anconeus

Long supinator

Long radial extensor
of the wrist and hand

Short radial extensor
of the wrist and hand

Common extensor of the fingers

Ulnar extensor of the wrist

Long abductor of the thumb

Short extensor of the thumb

Ligament of the wrist.

Tendon of the Long
extensor of the thumb

THE MUSCLES OF THE UPPER LIMB.
Lateral view.

SHORT RADIAL EXTENSOR OF THE WRIST AND HAND
(*Extensor carpi radialis brevior*)

This muscle comes next in order on the posterior region of the forearm. It arises from the external condyle of the humerus. The fleshy portion is suc-

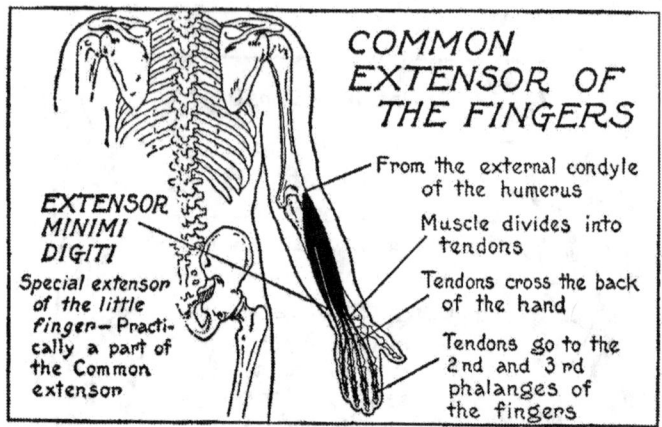

COMMON
EXTENSOR OF
THE FINGERS

From the external condyle
of the humerus

Muscle divides into
tendons

Tendons cross the back
of the hand

Tendons go to the
2nd and 3rd
phalanges of
the fingers

EXTENSOR
MINIMI
DIGITI

Special extensor
of the little
finger — Practi-
cally a part of
the Common
extensor

ceeded at the middle of the forearm by a tendon
that is inserted into the third metacarpal bone, or
that of the middle finger. Ordinarily this muscle
blends its form with adjacent parts, helping to fill
out the roundness of the region. If developed,
though, it may show as a relief limited by the surrounding forms.

The tendons of the two radial extensors of the
wrist and hand, before they reach their respective
insertions on the metacarpal bones, are crossed
obliquely by the fleshy portions of two thumb muscles and the tendon of another.

Both radial extensors, besides their functions as
specified by their names, abduct the hand in drawing it over as if trying to make the thumb touch
the side of the forearm.

COMMON EXTENSOR OF THE FINGERS
(*Extensor communis digitorum*)

Arising from the external condyle of the humerus, this muscle, its elongated relief usually conspicuous, passes down the middle of the back of the forearm. As the muscle nears the wrist, the fleshy portion divides into four parts, each of which becoming a tendon proceeds to the last phalanx of a finger. The relief of this muscle as it issues from a hollow —the condylar depression—directly over the external condyle, may be observed in action when moving the fingers in extension.   At the wrist, where the tendons diverge, a band of fibrous tissue—the posterior annular wrist ligament—passes over and holds these tendons in their places.   This strong ligament holds down the other extensor tendons, too.

Commonly the index, middle, and ring-finger tendons are more strongly marked as they cross the back of the hand than that of the little finger. This one can be observed, to be sure, but its relief is not so strongly evident.   Some of the tendons as they cross the back of the hand are united by small webs or slips, which in a sort of way makes it impossible to move certain fingers independently. The index-finger has a little more freedom of movement, as you can observe in your own hand.   The little finger, too, will perhaps have less restraint in its movements. Both of these digits have small special, or proper, extensors of their own. That of the little finger, the *extensor minimi digiti*, is only an offshoot of the common extensor; and the index-finger one, *extensor indicis*, although a sepa-

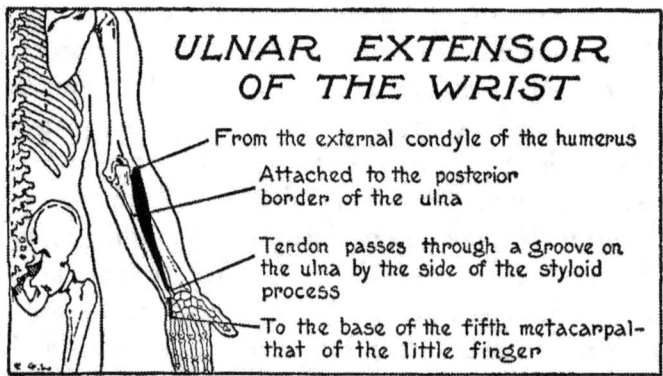

ULNAR EXTENSOR OF THE WRIST

From the external condyle of the humerus

Attached to the posterior border of the ulna

Tendon passes through a groove on the ulna by the side of the styloid process

To the base of the fifth metacarpal—that of the little finger

rate and deep-seated form, has its tendon in close contact with the tendon for the index-finger coming from the common extensor.

ULNAR EXTENSOR OF THE WRIST
(*Extensor carpi ulnaris*)

The last of the group of extensors that arises from the external region of the humerus. It passes on the back of the forearm, from its origin on the condyle, to be inserted into the fifth metacarpal bone, or that of the little finger. Its fleshy portion, a narrow relief on the inner side of the posterior region can be observed in action when the hand is bent back and the effort made to bear it over toward the ulnar side.

The ulnar extensor of the wrist constitutes one of the borders of the ulnar furrow, which furrow, a

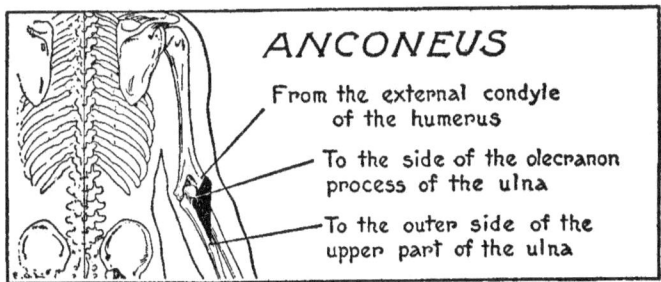

ANCONEUS

From the external condyle of the humerus

To the side of the olecranon process of the ulna

To the outer side of the upper part of the ulna

conspicuous depression extending the length of the forearm, follows the course of the subcutaneous edge of the ulna.

The next group of forearm muscles, those arising from the internal, or medial, condyle of the humerus, are flexors, and occupy in the main the anterior region. But before we proceed with their consideration, we note a small muscle that is placed at the back of the elbow.

ANCONEUS

This little muscle at the upper part of the forearm, close to the point of the elbow, is triangular in outline. It arises from the external condyle of the humerus and is inserted into the ulna on the outer side of the olecranon process. The fibres continue a short distance down along the border of the ulna. Its unmistakable relief of a triangular definition is

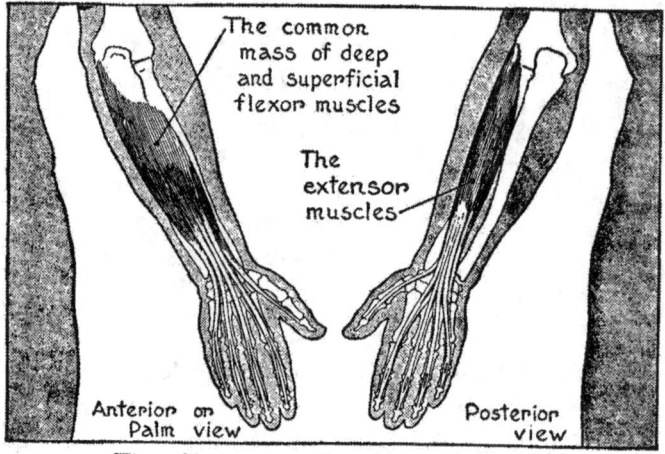

The common mass of deep and superficial flexor muscles

The extensor muscles

Anterior or Palm view

Posterior view

The flexors and extensors of the digits in antagonistic groups

clearly visible in the region which it covers. It is counted by anatomists as a prolongation of the triceps of the upper arm, and may be considered, too, as an auxiliary of this muscle in extending the forearm.

The placing of the forearm muscles into groups of flexors and extensors serves very well to illustrate the idea of antagonistic forms. The extensors on the posterior region, and the flexors on the anterior region, mainly, are more or less separated, even

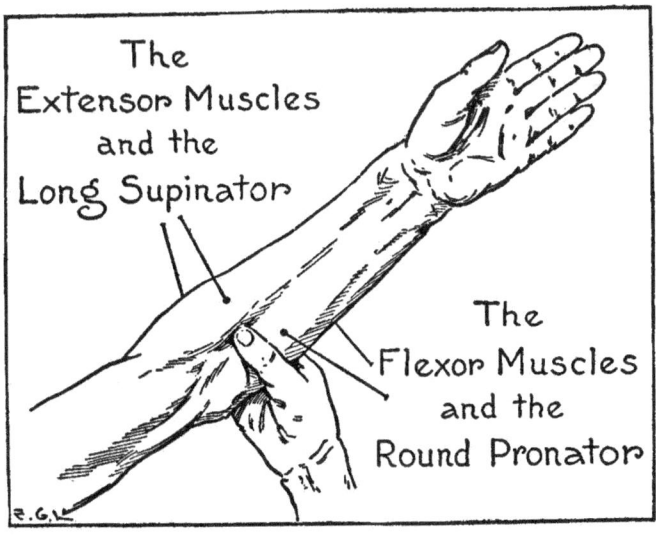

TO UNDERSTAND THE RELATIVE POSITIONS OF THE TWO GROUPS
OF FOREARM MUSCLES.

Place the fingers on the crest of the ulna and the thumb in the hollow of the elbow.
The hand now grasps one group. The muscles not so grasped belong to the
other group.

though the whole bulk of the forearm presents one undivided somewhat fusiform (spindle-shaped) structure.

One way by which we can grasp, in a double sense of the word grasp, the manner in which the two groups are disposed, is to encompass the inner side of the forearm with the digits of the opposite hand so that the fingers touch the subcutaneous edge of the ulna, and the thumb sinks into the hollow of the elbow.   Now the fingers and thumb will encircle the flexor muscles, including the round pronator, while all outside the grasp of the hand are the extensor muscles, including the long supinator.

ULNAR FLEXOR OF THE WRIST
(*Flexor carpi ulnaris*)

This muscle lies along the inner border of the ulnar furrow.   From the inner condyle of the humerus, where it arises, it proceeds along the inner side of the forearm to the wrist, where its tendon is attached to the pisiform bone.   At its upper part, besides the origin on the humerus, there are aponeurotic slips that find attachment to part of the ulna.   This muscle flexes the hand—bending it at the wrist, and slightly over toward the ulnar side.

The great bulk of the ulnar flexor of the wrist forms the principal part of the rotundity of the inner side of the forearm, and it gives the curve—we are thinking at this moment of its use to us in drawing—on the inner contour of the forearm when looked at both from the front and the back.

PALMARIS LONGUS

Among the cord-like tendons that will rise at the
front of the wrist during the flexing of the fingers
and bending of the hand, one perhaps will come out
very strongly, almost exactly in the middle of the

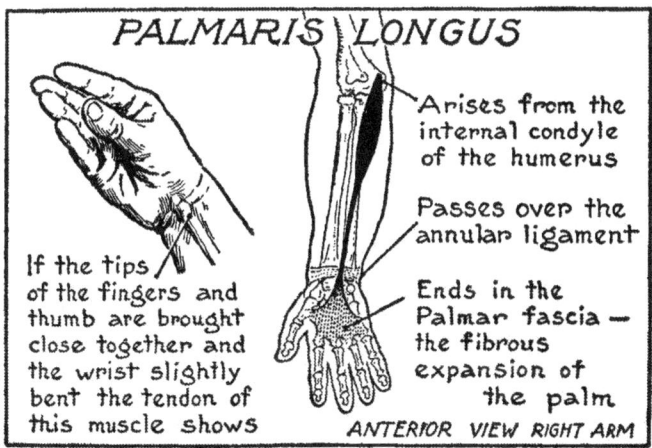

PALMARIS LONGUS

Arises from the
internal condyle
of the humerus

Passes over the
annular ligament

If the tips
of the fingers and
thumb are brought
close together and
the wrist slightly
bent the tendon of
this muscle shows

Ends in the
Palmar fascia —
the fibrous
expansion of
the palm

ANTERIOR VIEW RIGHT ARM

lower forearm. It will be, in all likelihood, the
tendon of the above-named muscle. It is possible,
though, that such a tendon does not spring out in
the particular wrist that is examined, as this muscular form is sometimes absent.

The palmaris longus is a thin muscle with a very
long slender tendon, arising from the inner condyle
of the humerus, continuing down the front of the

forearm to the middle of the wrist, and there to pass over the anterior annular wrist ligament. This wrist ligament is a strong band that passes over the various tendons of the flexor muscles, with the exception of this one, and holds them in their places as they cross this region.

A good way to show the tendon of the palmaris longus is to bring the tips of the thumb and fingers close together and, at the same time, bend the wrist slightly; the tendon then will come out into strong relief.

The palmaris longus is inserted into the palmar fascia, a fibrous expansion that stretches across the palm of the hand. The function of the muscle besides that of a flexor of the hand is to tighten this fibrous expansion on the palm.

RADIAL FLEXOR OF THE WRIST
(Flexor carpi radialis)

This muscle crosses the front of the forearm obliquely from its origin on the inner condyle of the humerus to the radial, or outer, side of the wrist, there it continues to an insertion into the base of the index-finger metacarpal. The fleshy portion of this muscle and the last two—ulnar flexor of the wrist and palmaris longus—combine to form the superficial convexity of the inner anterior region of the forearm.

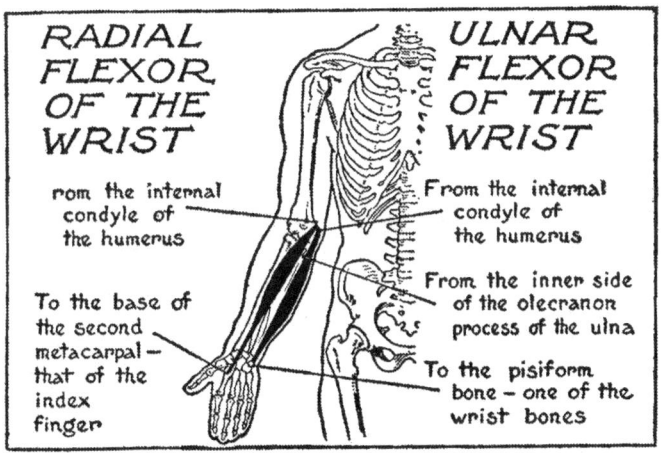

RADIAL FLEXOR OF THE WRIST

rom the internal condyle of the humerus

To the base of the second metacarpal — that of the index finger

ULNAR FLEXOR OF THE WRIST

From the internal condyle of the humerus

From the inner side of the olecranon process of the ulna

To the pisiform bone — one of the wrist bones

The tendon of the radial flexor of the wrist shows on the forearm, immediately above the ball of the thumb. It is close to this tendon, at the wrist toward the outer side, that the pulse is felt.

ROUND PRONATOR
(*Pronator radii teres*)

The surface muscle that first claimed our attention when we began the examination of the anatomy of the forearm was the long supinator. From it we encircled the general roundness of the forearm until we arrived at this form—the round pronator, the contiguous muscle of the long supinator. So we will have by the examination of this pronator completed our study of the surface anatomy of the main part of the forearm.

The round pronator arises from the inner condyle of the humerus and adjacent parts of the bone, fleshy fibres also touch the coronoid process of the ulna as they pass to the insertion into the outer edge of the radius. On the radius the fibres extend nearly to the middle of the shaft. On the outer form, the relief of the muscle is visible as it crosses the front of the forearm to be lost as it passes under the long supinator to its insertion on the radius. The round pronator is the antagonist of the long supinator, when this particular muscle operates in the manner that its name signifies.

SUPERFICIAL FLEXOR OF THE FINGERS
(Flexor digitorum sublimis—perforatus)

There are among the muscular forms within the general mass of the forearm two finger flexors, that help by their bulk to fill out the rotundity. One of these is called the superficial flexor of the fingers. It is not strictly superficial with respect to being placed next to the integument, only its lowermost tendons and slips of fleshy fibre betray their presence near the wrist in the intervals between other flexor tendons. It is called superficial in contradistinction to another finger flexor, which is a deepseated one.

The superficial flexor has an extensive origin, coming from the inner condyle of the humerus, the ulna, and from the radius. At the lower third of the forearm the muscle divides into four tendons, one

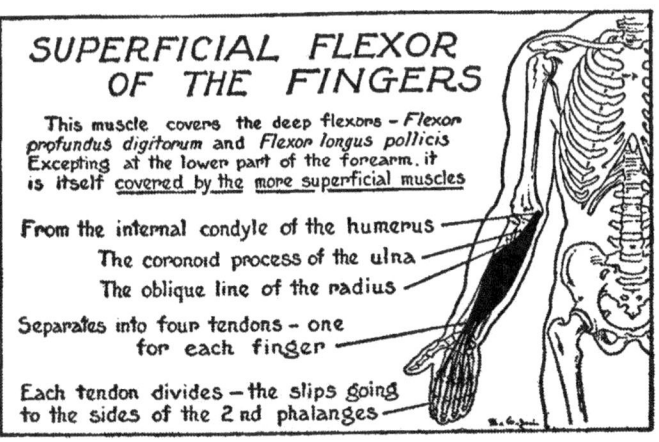

SUPERFICIAL FLEXOR
OF THE FINGERS

This muscle covers the deep flexors - *Flexor profundus digitorum* and *Flexor longus pollicis* Excepting at the lower part of the forearm, it is itself covered by the more superficial muscles

From the internal condyle of the humerus
The coronoid process of the ulna
The oblique line of the radius

Separates into four tendons - one for each finger

Each tendon divides - the slips going to the sides of the 2 nd phalanges

for each of the fingers. These pass together under the wrist ligament, and then diverge to their insertions into the second phalanges of the four fingers.

DEEP FLEXOR OF THE FINGERS
(*Flexor digitorum profundus—perforans*)

This flexor arises from the ulna and adjacent membranes. No part of its form is subcutaneous. It is noted here, in connection with the superficial flexor, on account of their sameness in function and the association of their tendons where they join the phalanges of the fingers. The singularly complicated way in which a pair of these tendons are attached to phalanges deserve a few words of description. The tendon of the superficial flexor (*perforatus*), which goes to the second phalanx, is provided with an aperture that is *pierced* by the underlying tendon of the deep flexor (*perforans*), which tendon after *piercing* the aperture in the superficial tendon goes forward to an insertion into the last phalanx.

LONG ABDUCTOR OF THE THUMB
(*Extensor ossis metacarpi pollicis*)
(*Abductor pollicis longus*)

The two thumb muscles, and the tendon of another, of which mention was made as crossing the tendons of the two radial extensors of the wrist and hand, now come under our notice.

On the back of the forearm, near the wrist, is a noticeable relief, set somewhat obliquely and tending toward the thumb. It is formed by the fleshy bodies and tendons of three thumb muscles. It must be first understood, however, in regard to them, that the greater part of their forms are covered by superficial muscles.

The long abductor, for instance, arises far up on the back of the shaft of the ulna, and the radius, and adjacent ligaments.   It is inserted by its long tendon into the base of the first metacarpal.   In action it pulls the metacarpal and, with it, the entire thumb away from the body of the hand.

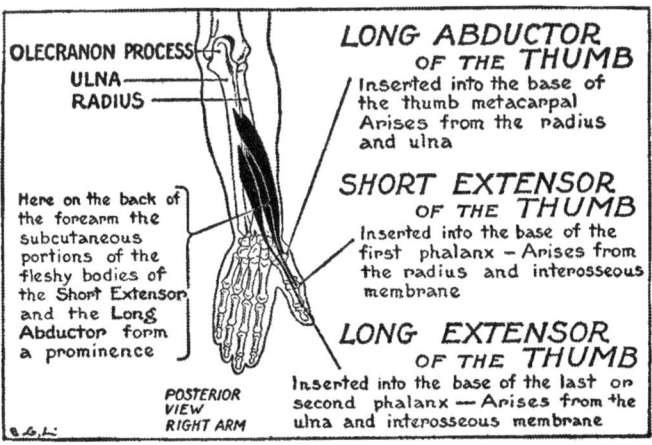

LONG ABDUCTOR *OF THE* **THUMB**
Inserted into the base of the thumb metacarpal
Arises from the radius and ulna

OLECRANON PROCESS
ULNA
RADIUS

SHORT EXTENSOR *OF THE* **THUMB**
Inserted into the base of the first phalanx — Arises from the radius and interosseous membrane

Here on the back of the forearm the subcutaneous portions of the fleshy bodies of the Short Extensor and the Long Abductor form a prominence

LONG EXTENSOR *OF THE* **THUMB**
Inserted into the base of the last or second phalanx — Arises from the ulna and interosseous membrane

POSTERIOR
VIEW
RIGHT ARM

THREE IMPORTANT THUMB MUSCLES.

SHORT EXTENSOR OF THE THUMB
(Extensor primi internodii pollicis)
(Extensor pollicis brevis)

This muscle comes from the inner border of the back of the radius and the adjacent membranes. It is inserted into the base of the first phalanx.   It pulls the thumb back—extension.

The lower parts of this thumb muscle, and the first enumerated, become subcutaneous as they

issue from the depth of the forearm, between the
diverging margins of the short radial extensor of
the wrist and hand and the common extensor of
the fingers.   Their combined mass in this region is
clearly perceptible on the form.   Its distinctive relief makes an important feature to observe in drawing—it varies the sweep of the forearm contour,
which we are so apt to think of as merely a simple
curve from the elbow to the wrist.

LONG EXTENSOR OF THE THUMB
(Extensor secundi internodii pollicis)
(Extensor pollicis longus)

This is placed lower on the forearm than the other
two, and its fleshy fibres are entirely covered by
superficial muscles.   The tendon only is visible under the integument.   It is inserted into the second,
or last, phalanx.   In forcible extension this tendon
shows as a prominent ridge along the back of the
thumb.   In extending the thumb, or thrusting it
away from the main bulk of the hand, note the
peculiar out-turning curve of the digit, and how
the curving is continued by the extra little bend of
the last phalanx.

One can distinguish in a sinewy hand, over the
outer posterior margin of the wrist, a small depression between the line of the long extensor tendon

and the combined line of the two other thumb-muscle tendons. This depression, made deeper by putting the muscles on a stretch, is called by the French

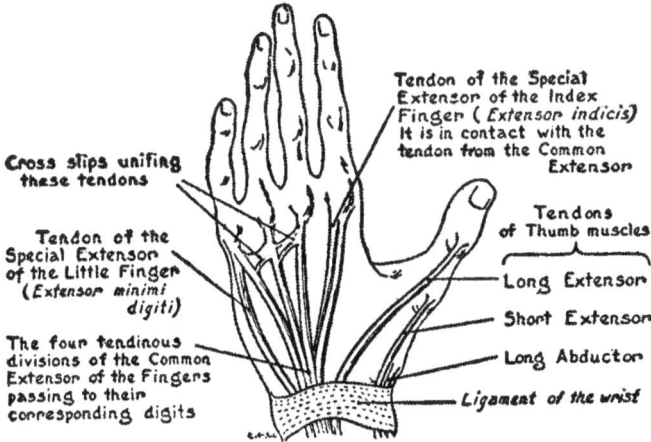

Tendon of the Special Extensor of the Index Finger (*Extensor indicis*) It is in contact with the tendon from the Common Extensor

Cross slips unifing these tendons

Tendon of the Special Extensor of the Little Finger (*Extensor minimi digiti*)

The four tendinous divisions of the Common Extensor of the Fingers passing to their corresponding digits

Tendons of Thumb muscles

Long Extensor

Short Extensor

Long Abductor

Ligament of the wrist

DIAGRAM TO SHOW THE GENERAL CHARACTER OF THE TENDONS ON THE BACK OF THE HAND.

the "tabatiere anatomique"; that is to say, the anatomical snuff-box.

THE HAND

As the skeletal plan of the hand is so easily perceived, the general idea of a hand is readily comprehended; but its complexity of joints and movements, with the resulting diversity of positions in which the hand can be put, makes it a hard member to draw. Its small muscles and tendinous slips, with other membranous parts, need not be studied in detail by the artist; he only needs to observe the general form as determined by the bones, and how the skeleton is filled out by the soft tis-

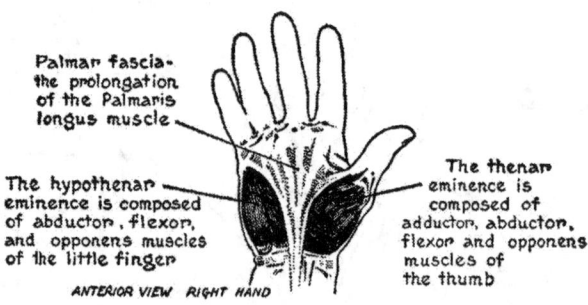

Palmar fascia-
the prolongation
of the Palmaris
longus muscle

The hypothenar
eminence is composed
of abductor, flexor,
and opponens muscles
of the little finger

The thenar
eminence is
composed of
adductor, abductor,
flexor and opponens
muscles of
the thumb

ANTERIOR VIEW   RIGHT HAND

THE MUSCLES OF THE BALL OF THE THUMB AND OF THE
EMINENCE ON THE LITTLE-FINGER SIDE OF THE PALM.

sues, and to note closely the character of such outer markings as cutaneous tendons, wrinkles, furrows, veins, and the web-like folds of skin in certain places.

On the palmar surface are two groups of muscles that should be attentively studied as to their general form. The larger group, a mass of muscles that pertains to the thumb, consists of a flexor and muscles that abduct, adduct, and pull the thumb over to lie across the palm and place it in an opposable position to the fingers. The fleshy prominence of the ball of the thumb is termed the thenar eminence. On the other side of the palmar surface is a lesser prominence, that of the little finger, or the hypothenar eminence. This is formed of muscles belonging to the little finger.

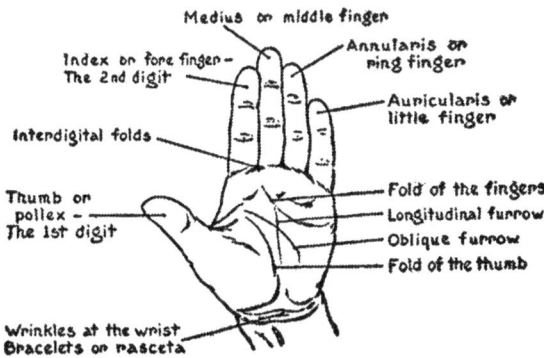

Medius or middle finger

Index or fore finger—
The 2nd digit

Annularis or
ring finger

Auricularis or
little finger

Interdigital folds

Thumb or
pollex —
The 1st digit

Fold of the fingers

Longitudinal furrow

Oblique furrow

Fold of the thumb

Wrinkles at the wrist
Bracelets or rasceta

NAMES OF DIGITS AND OF FOLDS AND FURROWS IN THE
SKIN OF THE PALM AND WRIST.

The artist should note, at the root of the hand, when drawing this member in any flexing position, the wrinkles that form across the front of the wrist. They are the rasceta, or bracelets.

The three interdigital clefts between the fingers are crossed by webs of skin. The apparent differences in the lengths in the fingers, whether viewed from the front or back, should be observed. On the back the clefts extend upward, toward the wrist, nearly to the large knuckle-joints, making the fingers from that side look longer than when viewed from the palmar side, where the webs of skin extend rather farther down—toward the finger-tips.

X

THE MUSCLES OF THE LOWER LIMB

The Thigh

TRICEPS FEMORALIS
(OR QUADRICEPS)

(Comprising the Rectus femoris and the two Vasti)

O N the front of the thigh, occupying the entire region, is the large muscular formation termed the triceps femoralis. It is made up of three muscles: the rectus femoris, the vastus externus, and the vastus internus. Sometimes this formation is designated as the *Quadriceps (four-headed) extensor cruris*. In this case, a deep-seated form that is closely united with one of the vastus muscles is counted as a separate and fourth division. In the triceps femoralis there is some little resemblance to the triceps of the arm. In both cases they are found on the first section of their respective limbs, and they are extensors of the next sections of those limbs. There is also a certain repetition in the way that the muscular divisions are arranged.

RECTUS FEMORIS

First we will consider the middle, or long portion the rectus femoris. The likeness in the placing of the triceps muscles in the two limbs is carried

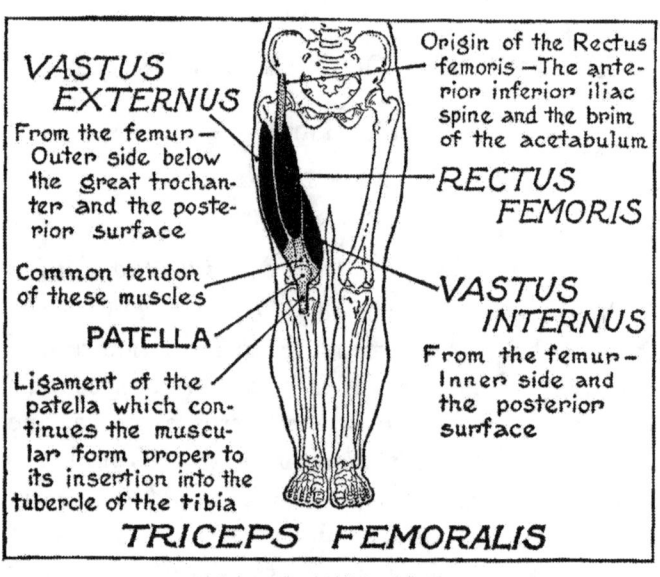

VASTUS
EXTERNUS
From the femur—
Outer side below
the great trochan-
ter and the poste-
rior surface

Common tendon
of these muscles

PATELLA

Ligament of the
patella which con-
tinues the muscu-
lar form proper to
its insertion into the
tubercle of the tibia

Origin of the Rectus
femoris —The ante-
rior inferior iliac
spine and the brim
of the acetabulum

RECTUS
FEMORIS

VASTUS
INTERNUS
From the femur—
Inner side and
the posterior
surface

TRICEPS FEMORALIS

ALSO CALLED THE *QUADRICEPS.*

out in that this long portion of the triceps femoralis takes origin from a girdle-bone—the ilium. The long portion of the triceps of the arm springs from, as we have learned, the important bone of the shoulder girdle—the scapula. Occupying the middle of the thigh, this division of the triceps of the thigh arises by a strong tendon from the lower anterior iliac spine, and from a point which is very close to the margin of the socket of the hip-joint. The fleshy portion is large and fusiform, the muscular fibres ending a short distance above the knee, where they join the common tendon of all three divisions. This tendon encloses within its fabric the patella, from which bone

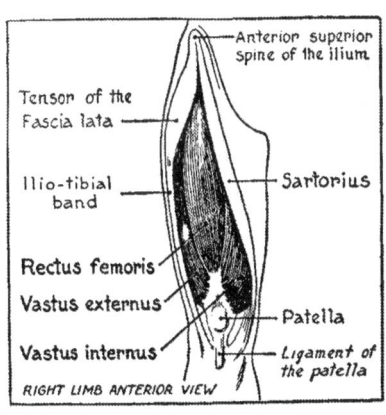

RIGHT LIMB ANTERIOR VIEW

HOW THE LARGE MUSCULAR MASS OF THE FRONT OF THE THIGH IS EN CLOSED BY OTHER FORMS

the tendinous part of the muscle is continued to the insertion into the tubercle of the tibia. This prolongation from the patella to the tubercle is more specifically named the ligament of the patella.

The lower margin of the fleshy part where the tendon begins is marked by a relief, while the tendon itself gives a somewhat flattened area immediately above the knee.

The rectus femoris gives, from the profile view, a definite front contour of the thigh, and its general convexity imparts form to the middle anterior region of the thigh.

The two vasti, the lateral divisions of the triceps of the thigh, arise from a limb-bone—the femur, a characteristic paralleling the manner of origin of the two lateral portions of the triceps of the arm, which also arise from a limb-bone—the humerus.

VASTUS EXTERNUS
(*Vastus lateralis*)

This division occupies the outer side of the thigh, extending its convexity around to the front to meet the margin of the rectus femoris, and to the back to the first posterior muscle. It arises from the femur near the base of the great trochanter, the edge of the linea aspera and adjacent surfaces of the bone. Its fibres as they near the knee pass into a flat tendon which joins the outer edge of the common tendon that goes to the patella.

VASTUS INTERNUS
(*Vastus medialis*)

This, the third division of the triceps femoralis, is placed farther down on the thigh than the other divisions. It arises from rather extensive areas on the shaft of the femur, and is inserted into the side of the patella and the common tendon. A matter

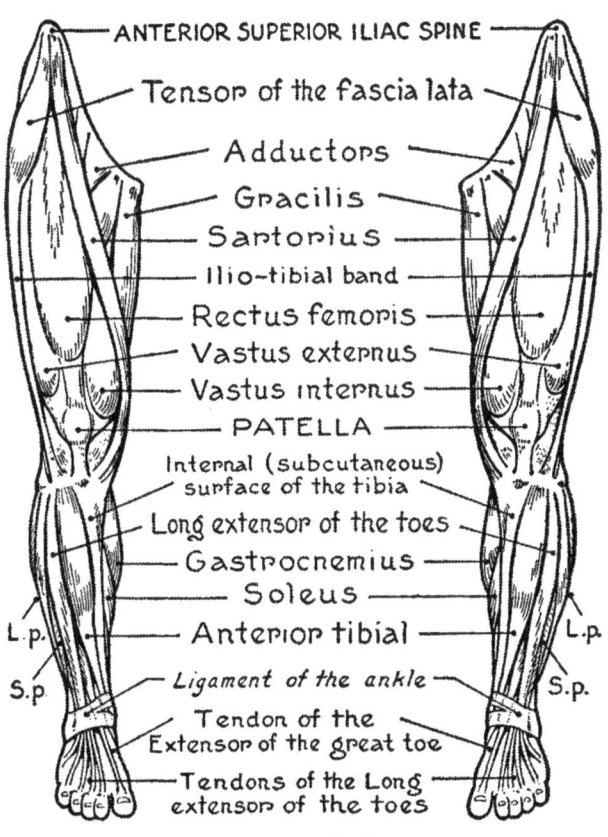

ANTERIOR SUPERIOR ILIAC SPINE

Tensor of the fascia lata

Adductors

Gracilis

Sartorius

Ilio-tibial band

Rectus femoris

Vastus externus

Vastus internus

PATELLA

Internal (subcutaneous)
surface of the tibia

Long extensor of the toes

Gastrocnemius

Soleus

Anterior tibial

L.p.

S.p.

Ligament of the ankle

Tendon of the
Extensor of the great toe

Tendons of the Long
extensor of the toes

L.p.

S.p.

L.p. Long peroneal   S.p. Short peroneal

THE MUSCLES OF THE LOWER LIMB.
Anterior view.

that should be especially noticed with respect to the vastus internus, on account of its being placed somewhat low on the thigh, is the boldness of the contour as the lower margin sweeps around the inner knee to the insertion into the side of the tendon. In the other vastus muscle—of the external side—the curvature of the form, as it extends to the region of the knee, is a gradual one.

Acting together, the three divisions of the triceps femoralis extend the leg on the thigh. The rectus femoris division, it should be observed, also has a supplementary function of flexing the thigh on the trunk, by virtue of its points of origin on the pelvic bone.

When the knee is bent the vasti muscles lose some of their characteristic curves at the knee, and then, as they are stretched out, allow the prominences of the tuberosities of the femur to be appreciable on the outer form.

TENSOR OF THE FASCIA LATA
(Tensor vaginæ femoris)
(Tensor fasciæ latæ)

This muscle is placed at the hip on the outer side of the thigh, extending from the anterior superior spine of the ilium obliquely downward to a point slightly below the level of the great trochanter of the femur. Here it is inserted into the fascia lata.

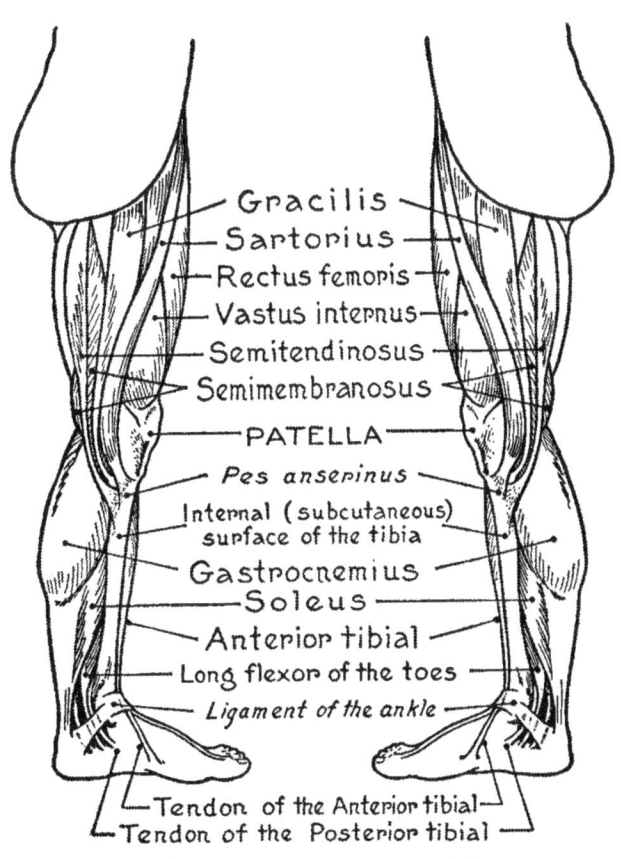

Gracilis

Sartorius

Rectus femoris

Vastus internus

Semitendinosus

Semimembranosus

PATELLA

Pes anserinus

Internal (subcutaneous) surface of the tibia

Gastrocnemius

Soleus

Anterior tibial

Long flexor of the toes

Ligament of the ankle

Tendon of the Anterior tibial

Tendon of the Posterior tibial

THE MUSCLES OF THE LOWER LIMB.

Inner view.

The fascia lata is a membrane that invests the region of the thigh and binds down the muscles there. The proper tendon of the muscle which we are considering is a thickened portion of this fascia

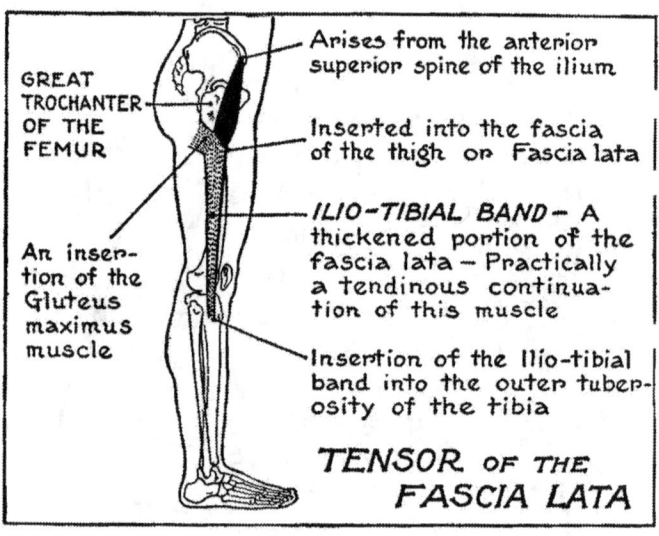

GREAT TROCHANTER OF THE FEMUR

Arises from the anterior superior spine of the ilium

Inserted into the fascia of the thigh or Fascia lata

ILIO-TIBIAL BAND — A thickened portion of the fascia lata — Practically a tendinous continuation of this muscle

An insertion of the Gluteus maximus muscle

Insertion of the Ilio-tibial band into the outer tuberosity of the tibia

TENSOR OF THE FASCIA LATA

that descends to the tibia at the outer side of the knee. It is called the ilio-tibial band, an important feature of the lateral region of the thigh. This fascial band is inserted into the external tuberosity of the tibia, near and on a level with the prominence of the head of the fibula. The lower part of the ilio-tibial band, when the muscle and fascia are in tension, shows as a slight ridge.

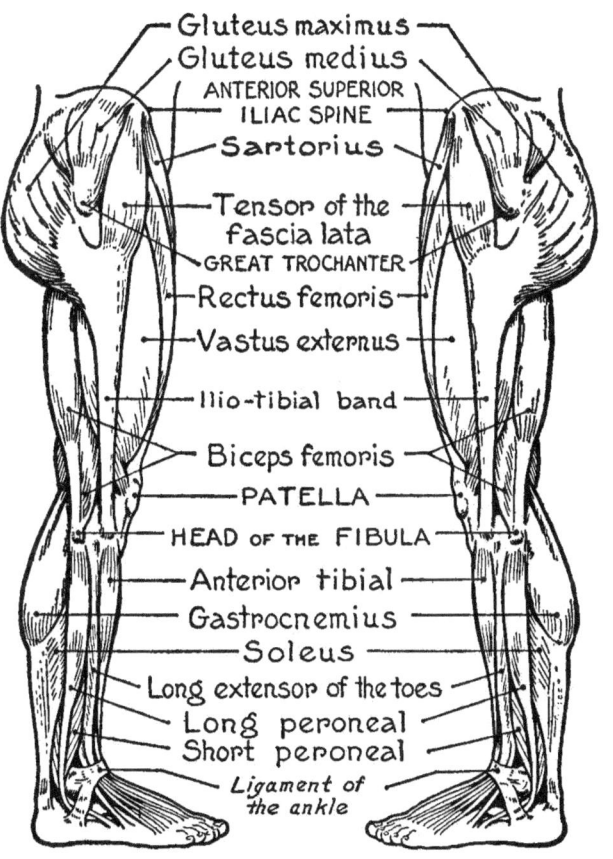

Gluteus maximus

Gluteus medius

ANTERIOR SUPERIOR
ILIAC SPINE

Sartorius

Tensor of the
fascia lata

GREAT TROCHANTER

Rectus femoris

Vastus externus

Ilio-tibial band

Biceps femoris

PATELLA

HEAD OF THE FIBULA

Anterior tibial

Gastrocnemius

Soleus

Long extensor of the toes

Long peroneal

Short peroneal

Ligament of
the ankle

THE MUSCLES OF THE LOWER LIMB.
Outer view.

The ilio-tibial band passes over and binds down the vastus externus. When this fascial band has been made taut, it causes a depression, very shallow, however, on the side of the thigh in the lateral mass of this vastus muscle.

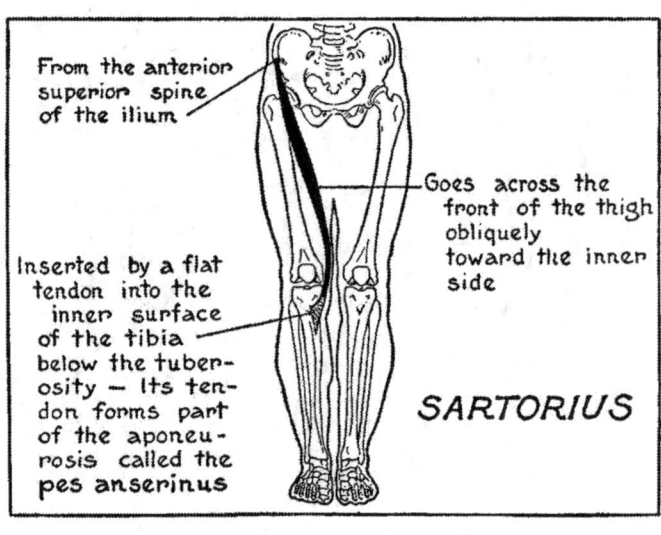

From the anterior superior spine of the ilium

Goes across the front of the thigh obliquely toward the inner side

Inserted by a flat tendon into the inner surface of the tibia below the tuberosity — Its tendon forms part of the aponeurosis called the pes anserinus

SARTORIUS

SARTORIUS

This is another muscle that arises from the anterior superior spine of the ilium. The other form, the tensor of the fascia lata, took a direction outward and downward, but the sartorius goes inward and downward. It is from within the angle made by these two muscles as they diverge from their

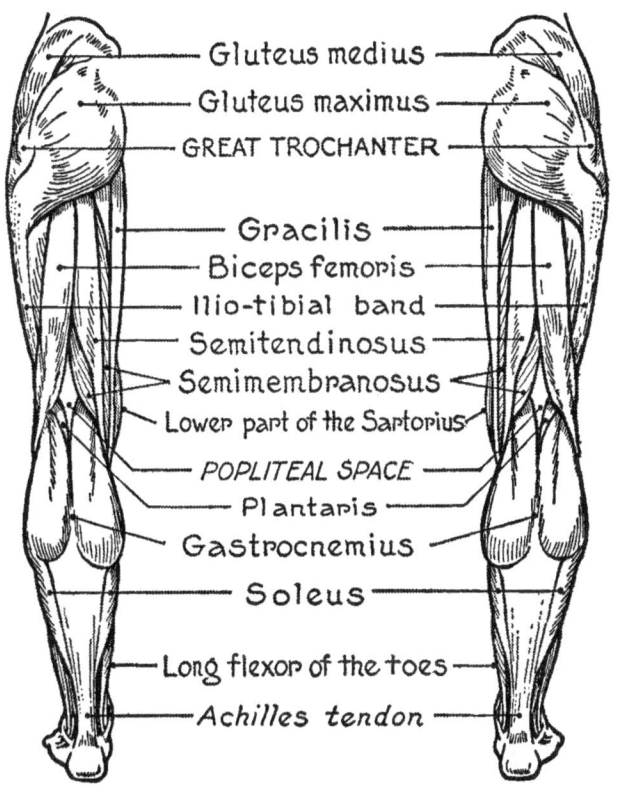

Gluteus medius

Gluteus maximus

GREAT TROCHANTER

Gracilis

Biceps femoris

Ilio-tibial band

Semitendinosus

Semimembranosus

Lower part of the Sartorius

POPLITEAL SPACE

Plantaris

Gastrocnemius

Soleus

Long flexor of the toes

Achilles tendon

THE MUSCLES OF THE LOWER LIMB.
Posterior view.

origins at the very top of the thigh that the rectus femoris proceeds from its origins on the hip-bone.

The sartorius goes obliquely downward, in a sinuous curve, across the thigh to the back of the knee, where it sweeps around the bony prominences of the articulation. A flattened tendon that here succeeds the fleshy portion goes forward to the inner surface of the tibia to be inserted close to the crest of the bone. This muscle, the longest in the body, follows in its course a sort of shallow trough.

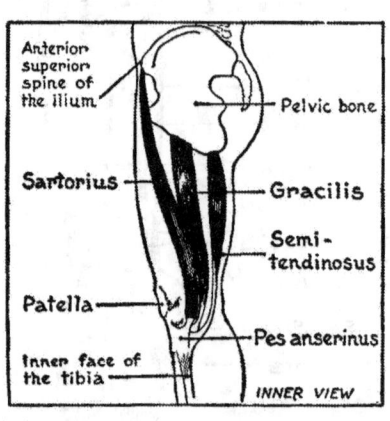

Anterior superior spine of the ilium

Sartorius

Patella

Inner face of the tibia

Pelvic bone

Gracilis

Semi-tendinosus

Pes anserinus

INNER VIEW

THE THREE THIGH MUSCLES THAT BLEND THEIR TENDONS TO FORM THE EXPANSION CALLED THE PES ANSERINUS.

If while standing on one leg the non-supporting leg is held out, the knees slightly bent and the femur rotated, that is, turned in its deep, cup-like joint, the sartorius will spring out into prominence. It then will be firm and tense, as it will be doing a great part of the work in maintaining the limb in this awkward position. The name sartorius was given to this muscle by the early anatomists because it appeared to them as the principal factor in putting the tailor's leg into that odd position in which he is seated atop the work-table (Latin, *sarcire*, to mend, patch).

GRACILIS

This form on the inner, or medial, side of the
thigh, is a long thin strip of muscle (Latin, *gracilis*,
slim, slender). It arises from the lower part of the
pelvic bone, close to the joining of the two pubic

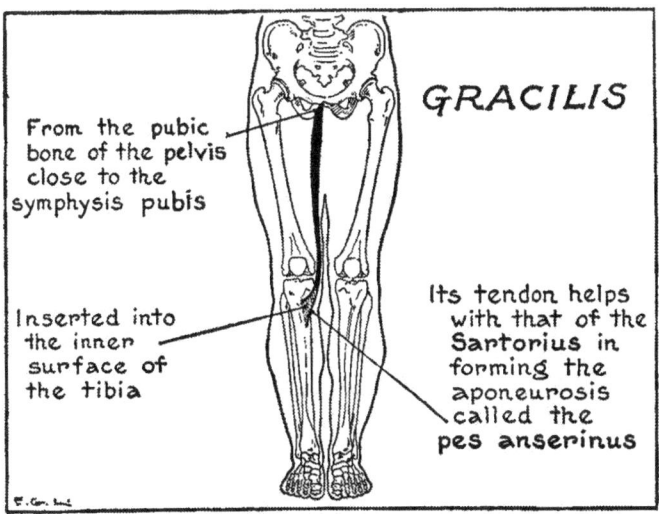

GRACILIS

From the pubic
bone of the pelvis
close to the
symphysis pubis

Inserted into
the inner
surface of
the tibia

Its tendon helps
with that of the
Sartorius in
forming the
aponeurosis
called the
pes anserinus

portions. From here it runs straight down, defining
the inner contour of the thigh, to the insertion into
the tibia on its inner surface below the knee.

The gracilis is an adductor of the thigh. Drawing the limbs together when they have been **spread
out** is effected by the gracilis muscles.

THE ADDUCTOR MUSCLES OF THE THIGH
(*Comprising the Pectineus, and the Adductor brevis, longus, and magnus*)

Viewed anteriorly, on the upper part of the thigh, we see a curvilinear triangular area bounded by the

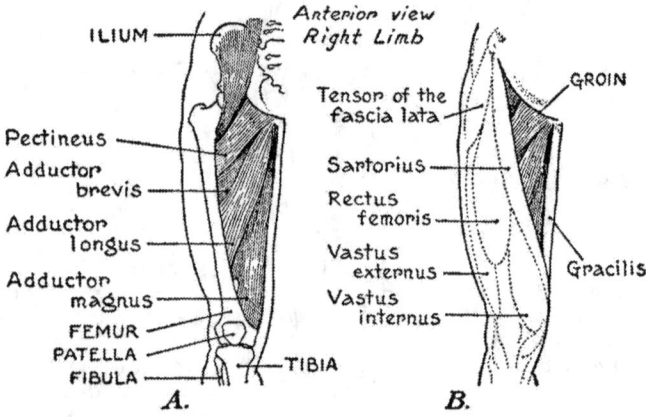

A. The pectineus and the adductor muscles of the thigh.
B. Their subcutaneous portions shown within the triangular area bounded by the gracilis and sartorius muscles and the groin.

sartorius, gracilis, and the fold of the groin. The adductor muscles lie within this area. There is no need for us to go into details in considering them, as they are of interest to us, as artists, principally in the matter of function as adductors, and that their aggregate mass fills out the form in the region.

These muscles pass from origins on parts of the pelvic bone to various parts of the femur. The general direction of the muscles and their fibres is a radiating one from the pelvic bone to insertions along the length of the femur.

THE THREE HAMSTRING MUSCLES

With these muscular forms, occupying the posterior femoral region, we complete our study of the muscular system of the thigh. All three forms coming under this specification have origins on the pelvis and are inserted into the leg-bones.

They all have the same functions —to bend the knee and flex the leg on the thigh, and also to draw the whole limb back.

Their superior extremities are covered by the gluteus maximus; and where they become visible in passing beyond the lower border of this muscle, they form one mass without any outwardly perceptible division. At about the middle of the thigh, however, a division

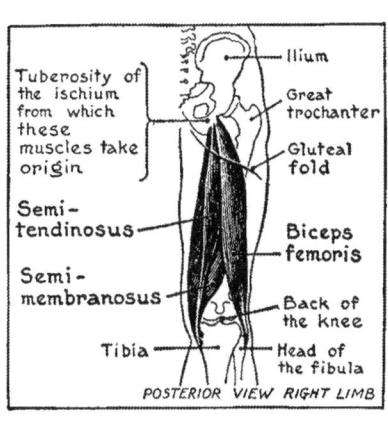

THE HAMSTRING MUSCLES.

occurs—one muscle continuing to the outer side, and the two others, in coterminous relationship, go to the inner side.

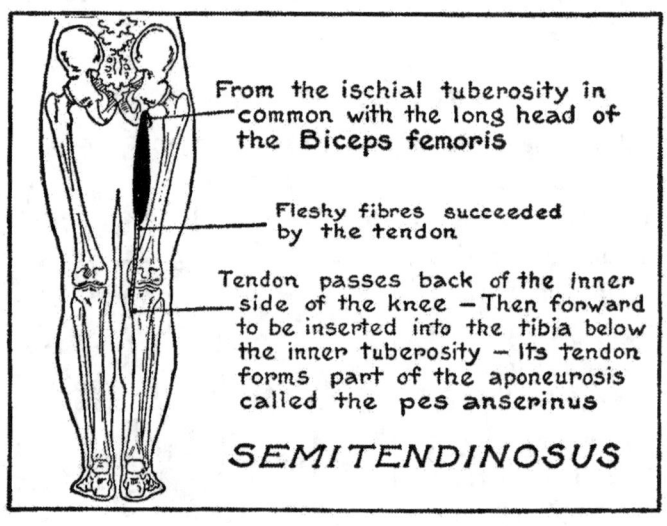

From the ischial tuberosity in common with the long head of the Biceps femoris

Fleshy fibres succeeded by the tendon

Tendon passes back of the inner side of the knee — Then forward to be inserted into the tibia below the inner tuberosity — Its tendon forms part of the aponeurosis called the pes anserinus

SEMITENDINOSUS

SEMITENDINOSUS

This muscle and the next one to be described, the semimembranosus, are the two hamstring muscles that go to the inner region of the back of the thigh. The semitendinosus arises from the ischial tuberosity of the pelvic bone, and is inserted into the inner side of the tibia immediately below the knee. At the place of insertion its expanded tendon forms with the tendons of the sartorius and the gracilis an intermingling of tissue called the pes anserinus (goose foot). The semitendinosus at its origin is closely associated with the other hamstring muscles. With the biceps femoris, the third of this group, it arises from the same point on the bone by a common tendon. The upper portion, about two-thirds or so, of the semitendinosus is composed of fleshy fibres, while below it is represented by a cord-like tendon that in certain actions of the knee can be perceived as a sharp ridge on the inner side of the lower thigh. This muscle lies over and covers part of the next muscle.

SEMIMEMBRANOSUS

This muscle arises from the ischial tuberosity of the pelvic bone above the common origin of the semitendinosus and the biceps femoris. Its insertion to bone is into the inner tuberosity of the tibia, rather toward the posterior surface. The tendon of insertion, moreover, gives off expansions that take part in the ligamentous joining of the knee-joint.

In general character, this muscle is tendinous at its extremities, with the middle portion composed of fleshy fibres. But the fleshy part descends somewhat close to the level of the back of the knee, where it gives form to the region.

The tendons of the semitendinosus and semi-

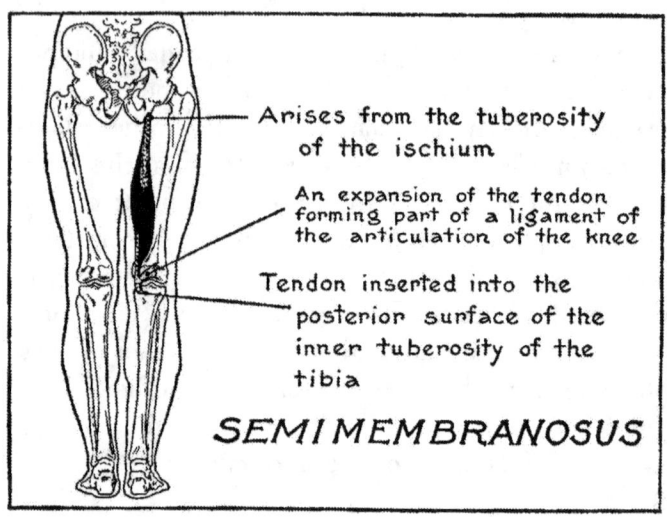

Arises from the tuberosity of the ischium

An expansion of the tendon forming part of a ligament of the articulation of the knee

Tendon inserted into the posterior surface of the inner tuberosity of the tibia

SEMIMEMBRANOSUS

membranosus (and to some extent those of the sartorius and gracilis) limit on the inner side the space on the back of the knee called the ham, or popliteal space. Outwardly this space is limited by the tendon of the next hamstring muscle to be considered.

BICEPS FEMORIS
(*Biceps flexor cruris*)

This muscle in certain respects has some resemblance to the biceps of the arm. Both arise by two heads, one long and the other short, and in both cases they are flexors of the particular limb to which

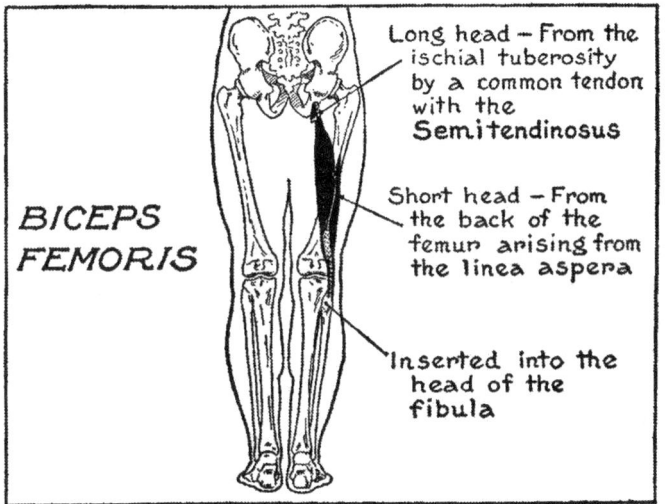

BICEPS
FEMORIS

Long head — From the
ischial tuberosity
by a common tendon
with the
Semitendinosus

Short head — From
the back of the
femur arising from
the linea aspera

Inserted into the
head of the
fibula

they belong.   The long head of this muscle comes
from the ischial tuberosity of the pelvic bone, while
the short head arises from the back of the femur.

The insertion is at the outer side of the knee,
where the tendon is attached to the head of the
fibula.   This latter point, as we learned in our study
of the skeleton of the lower limb, is a prominent
bony landmark of the region.

The biceps femoris is the only muscular form of
the external posterior region of the thigh, and it
alone forms the defining boundary of the popliteal
space on the outer side.   This space in certain stages
of flexion shows as a hollow, while in extension, or

the straightened limb, it has some degree of convexity.

A singular characteristic of the hamstring tendons is that they are too short to permit flexion of the thigh on the trunk when the knee is unbent; that is, if the entire lower limb is kept straight. This can be understood better by the individual experience of trying it yourself. Stand by the side of a table, or shelf, or where you can rest one hand for support. Now lift one leg from the floor and move it forward, keeping it stiff and without the least bending of the knee. See how far you can move it now. You will find that you cannot bring it even horizontally before you. After you have tried as hard as you can, suddenly bend the knee, and at once the thigh can be flexed and made to approach the front of the body.

The whole matter in this little experiment is that the much too short tendons were attached to the leg-bones in such a way that they prevented the limb from moving any farther. It was only when the knee was bent, so as to bring the points of attachment closer, and so shortening the distance and releasing the straining hamstring tendons.

The Leg and Foot

GASTROCNEMIUS AND SOLEUS

The calf of the leg is made up of the combined masses of the two muscles named above. The principal one, the gastrocnemius arises by two portions,

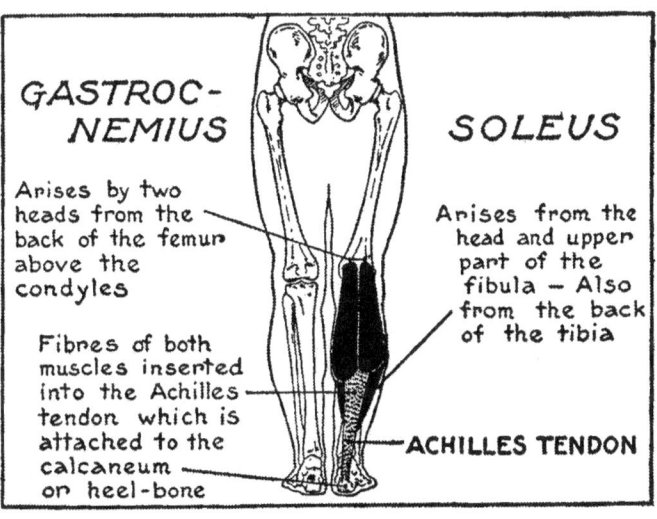

GASTROC-
NEMIUS

Arises by two
heads from the
back of the femur
above the
condyles

Fibres of both
muscles inserted
into the Achilles
tendon which is
attached to the
calcaneum
or heel-bone

SOLEUS

Arises from the
head and upper
part of the
fibula — Also
from the back
of the tibia

ACHILLES TENDON

or heads, from the back of the femur near the knee articulation. One head comes from above an outer, and another from an inner, condyle of that bone. The insertion is into the heel-bone, through the intermediary of that conspicuous membrane of the leg—the tendon of Achilles. The two heads of origin are at first separated, but soon become contiguous. Lower down they come into closer association to form the principal part of the bulky mass of the calf of the leg.

Where the muscle joins the tendon of Achilles, there is marked, especially when viewed in profile, that characteristic bulging of the region. In the case of a poorly developed calf, there is no perceptible break in the contour where the fleshy fibres are succeeded by the tendon. The level at which the fibres join the tendon varies according to the individual.

The gastrocnemius gives many defining outlines of the leg. Besides the profiles from the sides, its breadth of form gives the two lateral outlines as viewed posteriorly. And from the direct front view, the medial border shows its convexity as it defines the inner upper outline of the calf. It should be noted that the inner division of the gastrocnemius is larger and set on a lower level than the outer division. This has reference, especially with respect to the view of the muscle from the back.

The soleus, a flat muscle underlying the gastrocnemius, arises from the head and shaft of the fibula, and from the tibia. Its lower part, which is aponeurotic, joins the tendon of Achilles. Only the lateral borders of the muscle are subcutaneous, these showing on each side of the calf, immediately beyond the margins of the gastrocnemius.   When the muscle is put into tension they show as elongated reliefs.

The tendon of Achilles, that characteristic and distinguishing form of the lower leg, is broad where it receives the fleshy fibres of the calf muscles, tapers as it descends, and at the back of the ankle expands slightly before it joins the projection of the heel-bone.   It should be noted that fibres of the soleus join the sides of the heel tendon much farther down than the lowest margins of the gastrocnemius.

The calf muscles extend the foot by pulling on the heel-bone and bringing the foot in a straight line with the leg.   When acting alone, the gastrocnemius is, as can be well understood in considering the attachments to the femur, an accessory flexor of the leg on the thigh.   Calf muscles are brought into play during the various modes of progression and in maintaining the poise in standing on the toes.

The PLANTARIS is a small muscle, with a very long slender tendon, going from the femur to the heel-bone.   Its fleshy part joins and is somewhat combined with the bulk of the external head of the gastrocnemius.   The tendon passes through the mass of the leg, and then runs close to the inner edge of the tendon of Achilles.   It is a small formation and is to be considered as part of the general mass of the calf muscles.

ANTERIOR TIBIAL
(Tibialis anticus)

As referred to in the chapter on the skeleton of the lower limb, the inner subcutaneous surface of the tibia is a significant feature for the artist to note

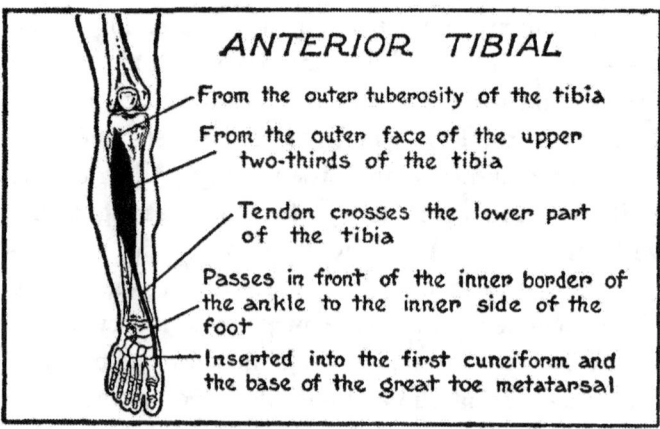

ANTERIOR TIBIAL

From the outer tuberosity of the tibia

From the outer face of the upper two-thirds of the tibia

Tendon crosses the lower part of the tibia

Passes in front of the inner border of the ankle to the inner side of the foot

Inserted into the first cuneiform and the base of the great toe metatarsal

in drawing. And it is of no less significance as an anatomical landmark in establishing the positions of neighboring muscles. For instance, to the outer side of its sharp crest, the anterior border, is the anterior tibial, an important leg muscle. Its fleshy body can be observed alternately swelling and relaxing when the foot is moved up (flexion) and down (extension).

The anterior tibial arises from the external tuberosity of the tibia, a part of its shaft, and adjoining membranes. It is inserted into the inner cuneiform—a tarsal bone, and also into the base of the metatarsal of the great toe. The course of the muscle, as can be seen by these attachments, is from the outer to the inner side of the leg. The passing from one side to the other taking place immediately above the ankle, where the tendon crosses the tibia to pass down on the inner border of the ankle and then under the arch of the foot to its insertions. The fleshy belly of the muscle, which extends from above to about the lower third of the leg, masks, or softens, the sharp crest of the tibia. The tendon shows as a very strong, thick cord where it crosses the lower front of the leg and ankle. In flexing the foot—moving its dorsum toward the front of the leg, this tendon comes out conspicuously. If with this flexion there is combined a lateral inward turning of the foot, the tendon can be further observed in movement.

At the bend of the ankle, a strong band, the annular ligament of the ankle, binds down the tendon of the anterior tibial as it crosses the region. Other tendons belonging to the extensor muscles (to be considered directly) are also held in place by this ligament as they cross the ankle.

EXTENSOR OF THE GREAT TOE
(*Extensor proprius pollicis pedis*)
(*Extensor hallucis longus*)

While putting the foot into action so as to bring into prominence the tendon of the anterior tibial, you no doubt noticed another tendon on the back

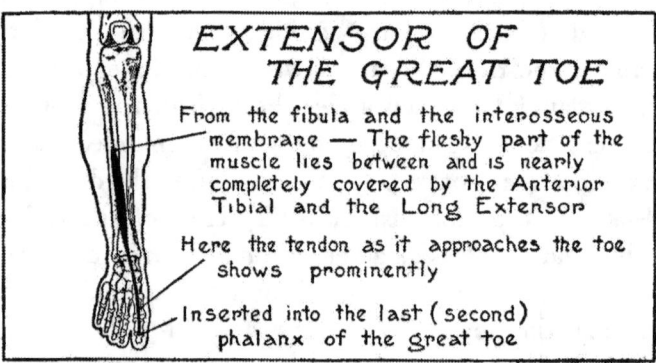

EXTENSOR OF
THE GREAT TOE

From the fibula and the interosseous membrane — The fleshy part of the muscle lies between and is nearly completely covered by the Anterior Tibial and the Long Extensor

Here the tendon as it approaches the toe shows prominently

Inserted into the last (second) phalanx of the great toe

of the foot going directly to the middle line of the great toe. This is the tendon of the special, or proper, extensor of the great toe. It can be brought out into very strong relief if the toe is extended; that is, if the effort is made to bring the toe back in the direction of the dorsum of the foot.

The extensor of the great toe arises from the middle of the shaft of the fibula and the interosseous membrane. Its fleshy portion is covered by the anterior tibial and the next form to be noticed, the long extensor of the toes.   The tendon appears as an external marking at the divergence of the last two named muscles, at about the lower third of the leg.   Then after passing under the ligament of the ankle, it crosses the top of the foot to an insertion into the last phalanx of the great toe.   Where this tendon passes lengthwise on the dorsum of the foot it marks the highest elevation of the instep and is, in this way, an important detail to heed in drawing. On the outer side of the line of this tendon, the surface of the foot slopes gradually toward the little toe side; while on the inner side it pitches abruptly to the vault, or arch, of the foot.

A matter with respect to the action of this muscle should be noted: although its function is, as its name implies, an extensor, if the same pull on the muscle that extends the toe be continued, flexion of the foot will result; that is to say, the foot will be drawn toward the front of the leg.

LONG EXTENSOR OF THE TOES
(Extensor longus digitorum pedis)

This muscle lies on the outer side of the leg bordering the anterior tibial.   The fleshy parts of both muscles are more or less associated in the matter of giving form to that region.

The long extensor of the toes arises from the

outer tuberosity of the tibia, part of the fibula, and adjacent membranes. It is inserted by four tendinous divisions into the four outer toes; that is, from the second to the last. The tendons diverge from the muscle at the lower part of the leg near

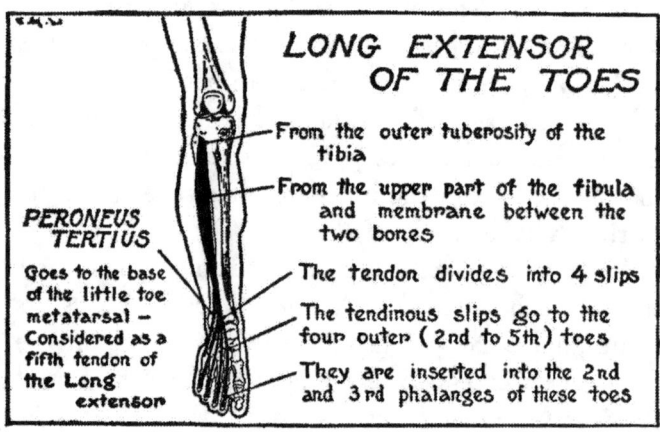

LONG EXTENSOR OF THE TOES

From the outer tuberosity of the tibia

From the upper part of the fibula and membrane between the two bones

The tendon divides into 4 slips

The tendinous slips go to the four outer (2nd to 5th) toes

They are inserted into the 2nd and 3rd phalanges of these toes

PERONEUS TERTIUS

Goes to the base of the little toe metatarsal — Considered as a fifth tendon of the Long extensor

the ankle, and after passing under the ankle ligament, go fan-like to their insertions on the second and third phalanges of their respective toes. Where the tendons cross the dorsum of the foot they show as sinewy prominences, especially when the muscle contracts during the operation of its proper function—extension of the toes. The line of the little-toe tendon should be particularly observed, as it defines the place where the plane of that side of the foot changes its direction and slopes toward the border of the foot that is in contact with the ground.

A small muscle that is considered as an accessory, or a fifth tendon, of the long extensor of the toes, is the PERONEUS TERTIUS.   At first its tendon passes by the side of the little-toe tendon of the long extensor, but after issuing from beneath the ankle ligament, it turns off to the base of the fifth metatarsal bone.   The origin of this muscle is closely associated with that of the long extensor of the toes.

LONG PERONEAL
(Peroneus longus)

With the enumeration of the long and the short peroneal muscles we have completed the list of the important—near-to-the—surface muscles of the leg. The long peroneal is situated on the outer side of the leg between the long extensor of the toes and the soleus.   It arises from the head and upper part of the fibula and adjoining membranes.   The elongated fleshy portion, extending to about the middle of the leg, where it is succeeded by a long slender tendon that continues to the ankle, passes around its prominence, or the malleolus, after which it goes under and across the foot to be inserted into the base of the great-toe metatarsal bone, and by a slight attachment to a neighboring tarsal bone.

The peculiar course of the long peroneal muscle and tendon should be well understood—originating from the outer side and ending on the inner side.

The principal function of the long peroneal is to extend the foot; but it can be seen by the course of

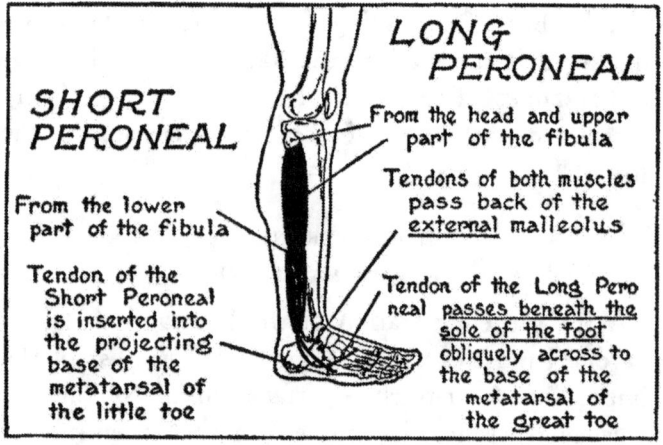

its tendon, across the sole of the foot, that in strong action it turns this sole outwardly.

As ordinarily developed, this muscle forms part of the general roundness of the leg that begins at the anterior tibial and continues on the outer side to the reliefs of the soleus and the gastrocnemius. The tendon, though, is a very significant feature of the region of the leg directly above the outer malleolus. It forms that sharp ridge which is observable there, and which in the model shows as an eminence dividing one side that catches a plane of light from another that is, more or less, in shadow.

SHORT PERONEAL
(*Peroneus brevis*)

The tendon of this muscle also takes part in the formation of the characteristic ridge above the ankle, and adds to the prominence of the malleolus of that side. It arises from the lower two-thirds, or so, of the fibula. The fibres are covered, in the main, by those of the long peroneal. Some of the lower fibres only are subcutaneous. The tendon, after passing around the malleolus, turns in the direction of the little-toe metacarpal, where it is inserted into its prominent projecting base. The short peroneal helps in the extension of the foot.

POSTERIOR TIBIAL
(*Tibialis posticus*)

LONG FLEXOR OF THE TOES
(*Flexor longus digitorum pedis*)

The inner malleolus has, too, certain tendinous forms that pass around and accentuate its prominence. They come from deep muscles of the leg that show but little of their parts subcutaneously.

The anatomical plan of the inner region of the leg, thinking of it now as a mere diagram, is very simple; there is first the inner surface of the tibia, next parts of the soleus and gastrocnemius muscles, and then the tendon of the heel. Now, in the remain-

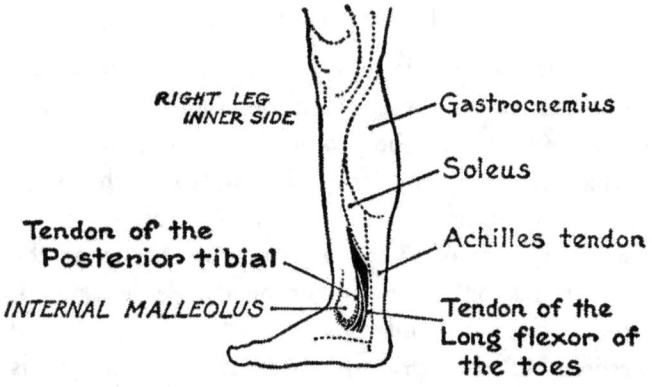

RIGHT LEG
INNER SIDE

Gastrocnemius

Soleus

Tendon of the
Posterior tibial

Achilles tendon

INTERNAL MALLEOLUS

Tendon of the
Long flexor of
the toes

THE TENDONS OF TWO DEEP LEG MUSCLES THAT SHOW ON THE INNER REGION OF THE ANKLE.

ing very small space above the prominence of the malleolus, the tendons and a few fibres of some of the deep muscles of the leg disclose themselves. Two of these forms are the muscles named at the head of this paragraph. One of these, the posterior tibial, has its tendon only close to the skin, the fleshy part lying solely within the depth of the leg, where it arises from the bones and adjacent mem-branes. The tendon joins, under the foot, certain of the tarsal bones. This muscle helps to extend the foot and turn it so that the sole faces inward.

The other muscle, the long flexor of the toes, shows a small portion of its fleshy part under the skin; its tendon, going downward, passes by the side of that of the posterior tibial in turning around the inner malleolus.

The tendons, only, of these two muscles interest us, as they are the only parts of their forms that have any direct modification on the external relief. Their combined form is plainly perceived immediately above the bony projection of the inner malleolus as a slightly ridged elevation. As a relief it is not so sharply defined, nor as large as the peroneal tendinous prominence of the outer side of the ankle.

SHORT EXTENSOR OF THE TOES
(*Extensor brevis digitorum pedis*)

On the dorsum of the foot, the only fleshy parts of any muscular form are those of the short extensor of the toes. It arises on the outer side of the foot, from the forepart of the heel-bone. The muscle divides into four slips, which taper into tendons going to the first (great toe), second, third, and fourth toe-bones. The muscle gives to the outer surface a discernible convexity on the foot

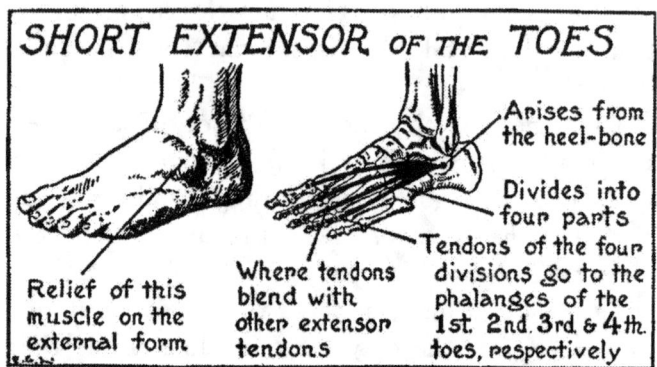

SHORT EXTENSOR OF THE TOES

Arises from the heel-bone

Divides into four parts

Tendons of the four divisions go to the phalanges of the 1st. 2nd. 3rd. & 4th. toes, respectively

Where tendons blend with other extensor tendons

Relief of this muscle on the external form

below, and immediately before, the ankle-joint. The fibrous slips and tendons of this short extensor pass obliquely under the tendons of the long extensor of the toes.

THE SOLE

On the under side, or plantar region, of the foot are found, besides the tendons of leg muscles, a number of shorter forms that move (in the natural foot, uncramped by foot-gear) the toes. These have in their attachments and functions like qualities to the similar forms of the hand. But as they have no influence on the surface contours, there is no need here for any detailed study of their peculiarities. With the cushions of fatty tissue and the dense membranes of the sole, their fleshy parts and tendons do, to be sure, help to fill out the form. And this form is kept in shape by the thick integument that invests the region, rounds off the lateral margins, and extends from the heel to the toes.

INDEX

INDEX

www.ingramcontent.com/pod-product-compliance
Lightning Source LLC
Chambersburg PA
CBHW071253220526
45468CB00001B/104